Crosscurrents / MODERN CRITIQUES

Harry T. Moore, *General Editor*

The Early Tales
of Henry James

James Kraft

WITH A PREFACE BY

Harry T. Moore

SOUTHERN ILLINOIS UNIVERSITY PRESS
Carbondale and Edwardsville

FEFFER & SIMONS, INC.
London and Amsterdam

Quotations from *The Art of the Novel: Critical Prefaces by Henry James*
Reprinted by permission of the publisher, Charles Scribner's Sons

Quotations from *The Selected Letters of Henry James*
Copyright © 1955 by Leon Edel
Reprinted by permission of William Morris Agency, Inc.

Contents

Chronology of the Early Tales

All the tales originally appeared in magazines. Those starred (twenty-one) were republished in book form by James. Those double starred (eight) were also selected by James for the New York Edition of his works.

Preface

It was inevitable that this series should one day have a book on Henry James, for he is regarded not only as a highly important author, but also this particular editor is a Henry James enthusiast. And James Kraft has given us just the kind of book we needed, a thorough survey of James's early stories and short novels.

Some of us can remember a time when James was not regarded so highly. Even in the 1920's, when literary craftsmanship was so well thought of, readers neglected James. He had also been generally neglected during his own lifetime, except for Daisy Miller in 1878. In the last years of his life the collected editions of his work didn't have impressive sales, and after his death in 1916 he was remembered chiefly as "the novelist's novelist," still largely unread. Oddly enough, the change came in the 1930's, when so many readers were absorbed by proletarian novels. In 1934 the Henry James number of Hound and Horn helped bring him to attention; in it, Edmund Wilson and other important writers treated James seriously indeed. Robert Cantwell wrote persuasively of him in the New Republic, and the James centennial issue of the Kenyon Review helped further in 1943. Perhaps the war then going on aroused still further interest in James's "international theme." Anyhow, by the end of the war the revival was on in full force, and now James is regarded as a world author of magnitude.

Some readers, however, care little for his last period, in the early twentieth century; they think that he became supersubtle and that his language became too tenuous. But others of us like those last books and join F. O. Matthiessen in thinking that they constitute James's "major phase." This doesn't mean that we who prefer those last books don't think well of the earlier work; indeed, we enjoy finding in it many of the seeds that were to blossom later.

And it is with such seeds that Mr. Kraft is concerned in the present book. He looks thoroughly at that early work of James, from the first slight stories to "A Bundle of Letters," which appeared in 1879, the year before The Portrait of a Lady offered the first emphatic testimony of James's true greatness. Mr. Kraft deals with thirty-seven stories in all, giving us a fresh view of the developing writer.

He is often synoptic, but so is much other excellent criticism; Edmund Wilson, for example, is a master of the method. The way a man describes a story is in itself a form of criticism. Mr. Kraft gives us the embodiment of these early tales of James, but always significantly points out the prototypes for later characters, the birth and growth of themes to be subsequently expanded. Above all he shows us, through James's evolving sense of morality, the development of his artistic vision. Readers not well acquainted with James's earlier work will find this book an impressive guide to it, while even those who know James from beginning to end will find Mr. Kraft's examination of this early material extremely useful.

HARRY T. MOORE

Southern Illinois University
April 26, 1969

Introduction

There are one hundred and twelve tales by Henry James, varying in length from a few thousand words to over forty thousand. The first appeared in February, 1864, when James was twenty; the last in April–May, 1910, when he was within six years of his death at the age of seventy-two. Tales were written in all periods of his life and represent all styles of his art. They were usually first published in magazines; some were rewritten and republished in volumes of tales; fifty-five were rewritten for the 1907–09 New York Edition of James's works that he selected and edited; forty more appeared in the novels and stories edited by Percy Lubbock in 1921–23. The entire collection of tales was made available for the first time in *The Complete Tales of Henry James* that began to appear in 1962.[1]

Almost half the volumes of the New York Edition are devoted to the tales, and nine Prefaces, half the total James wrote, discuss his short fiction. These Prefaces reveal the extreme pleasure he took in this fiction and the conscious artistry he gave to its composition. He called his interest "great" and "from far back" in the "whole 'question of the short story,' "[2] and makes clear he is as much a writer of tales as of novels.

The tale is for James usually defined as a picture or an anecdote. He uses the generic terms "tale" and "short story" interchangeably for these but prefers the term "tale." The distinction is delicate between the picture and the anecdote, and he admits that "a given attempt may place itself near the dividing-line" between them.³ A picture he defines as a limited study, yet within its small area one that James says he revels in. The picture is always

> aiming at those richly summarised and foreshortened effects—the opposite pole again from expansion inorganic and thin—that refer their terms of production, for which the magician has ever to don his best cap and gown, to the inner compartment of our box of tricks.⁴

The anecdote is an idea that is too complex for this small canvas of the picture, yet is only directed toward a single character and situation.

> The anecdote consists, ever, of something that has oddly happened to some one, and the first of its duties is to point directly to the person whom it so distinguishes. He may be you or I or any one else, but a condition of our interest—perhaps the principal one—is that the anecdote shall know him, and shall accordingly speak of him, as its subject.⁵

James objects in either case to the limiting of a tale to a certain length. The length of a tale is determined by what its telling demands, not by any prescription.

> The forms of wrought things . . . *were*, all exquisitely and effectively, the things; so that, for the delight of mankind, form might compete with form and might correspond to fitness; might, that is, in the given case, have an inevitability, a marked felicity. . . . Shades and differences, varieties and styles, the value above all of the idea happily *developed*, languished, to extinction, under the hard-and-fast rule of the "from six to eight thousand words"—when, for one's benefit, the rigour was a little relaxed. For myself, I delighted in the shapely *nouvelle*—as, for that matter, I

had from time to time and here and there been almost encouraged to show.[6]

The *nouvelle*—a form he describes as "our ideal, the beautiful and blest" [7]—he takes from the French; its flexibility does not necessitate for James the restrictions in length (hence, in depth of treatment) that he feels apply to the English terms "short story" or "tale," although for James the *nouvelle* is *not* a short novel. *The Reverberator* (fifty-five thousand words) he calls a short novel,[8] but "The Coxon Fund" (twenty-five thousand words) he calls a *nouvelle*.

> A marked example of the possible scope, at once, and the possible neatness of the *nouvelle*, it takes its place for me in a series of which the main merit and sign is the effort to do the complicated thing with a strong brevity and lucidity—to arrive, on behalf of the multiplicity, at a certain science of control. Infinitely attractive—though I risk here again doubtless an effect of reiteration—the question of how to exert this control in accepted conditions and how yet to sacrifice no real value; problem ever dearest to any economic soul desirous to keep renewing, and with a frugal splendour, its ideal of economy.[9]

It should be emphasized that for James the tale could be whatever he created as long as it is not so extended and inclusive as to enter the complexity and breadth of the novel. The important concern for the short fiction is its economy of purpose. The richness of insight possible *within* this economy makes the tale fascinating to James.

> To improvise with extreme freedom and yet at the same time without the possibility of ravage, without the hint of a flood; to keep the stream, in a word, on something like ideal terms with itself: that was here my definite business. The thing was to aim at absolute singleness, clearness and roundness, and yet to depend on an imagination working

freely, working (call it) with extravagance; by which law it wouldn't be thinkable except as free and wouldn't be amusing except as controlled.[10]

This statement refers to the form of his short fiction, but it can also be read as a figurative statement of what James is expressing in this fiction. As he wants to write with freedom *and* control, he also desires to describe life lived freely but with conscious control. James comments in one Preface on "the movement of life," [11] a phrase meant to express the degree to which what is experienced is subtly felt by the individual and allowed to vibrate in his life. A person who has neither felt finely nor allowed these feelings to affect his life would be someone for James who has not lived, to whom nothing has happened. One must be free to act, to experience, "with extravagance," but one must be controlled as well or the experience will not be felt. For James "the thing of profit is to *have* your experience—to recognize and understand it, and for this almost any will do; there being surely no absolute ideal about it beyond getting from it all it has to give." [12]

What it means to James to "live life" is called by Marius Bewley "the one great overwhelming problem that most of his characters have to face sooner or later, in one way or another." [13] James portrays "the movement of life" through what he calls "the mixture of manners," [14]—the human actions, the social gestures, the dramatic situations through which one can morally interpret life.

The mixture of manners was to become in other words not a less but a very much more appreciable and interesting subject of study. The mixture of manners was in fine to loom large and constantly larger all round; it was to be a matter, plainly, about which the future would have much to say. Nothing appeals to me more, I confess, as a "critic

of life" in any sense worthy of the name, than the finer-
if indeed thereby the less easily formulated—group of the
conquests of civilization, the multiplied symptoms among
educated people, from wherever drawn, of a common intelligence and a social fusion tending to abridge old rigours
of separation.[15]

To be this critic of life by being an interpreter of its
marvelous and complex morality of manners is James's
purpose in writing. He continually refines his style to become a clearer interpreter. Eventually he sees the finest
experiences of life as those set and controlled within art.

A study of only the first thirty-seven of the one hundred and twelve tales of Henry James is naturally limited,
but by concentrating on his earliest short fiction and re-
lating it to his other work, written at the same time and
later, it is possible to gain a clearer understanding of the
foundations of James's fiction and to suggest the evolution of his art. The short fiction is where one can best
study this evolution, for James was slow to write long
fiction. He was to write tales for seven years before attempting a novel; then wait another four years before
writing his second; and not until 1880, sixteen years after
he had begun to write, was he to create his first major
work, *The Portrait of a Lady*. By 1880 he had also written "Madame de Mauves," "Daisy Miller," and "An International Episode," as well as several lesser known but
distinctive tales—thirty-seven in all.

Any writing on the early work of James is indebted to the
study made in 1930 by Cornelia Pulsifer Kelley, *The
Early Development of Henry James*. My work, as hers,
stops with the publication of *The Portrait of a Lady* in
1880, but differs from hers in its concentration on the
tales. It also differs in that my comments can benefit
from the scholarship since 1930, particularly that by

Leon Edel. His edition of the complete tales is used here, and because it is thematically satisfactory, each of the four chapters corresponds to the tales in one of the first four volumes of the *Complete Tales*.

JAMES KRAFT

April 1969
Middletown, Connecticut

1

The Apprentice Years—Life in America: 1864–1868

The United States is the setting for ten of the first eleven tales Henry James wrote between 1864 and 1868. The one exception is "A Tragedy of Error" (1864), his earliest known work. Set in a French seaport, this tale is a lurid and fanciful melodrama of adultery and murder. Into the passionate French scene the young writer—not yet twenty-one—interjects his cool authorial voice, as he is so often to do in later fiction: "My story begins with a gentleman coming out of the office and handing her a letter" (I, 23); and he hesitantly moves toward the detached, third-person observer he is frequently to use: "if for any reason a passer by had happened to notice her" (I, 29).[1] The tale is, however, noticeably out of place among James's earliest fiction and was probably written under the influence of Balzac.[2] In the next ten tales set in his native land, James examines people and places he better understands from experience.

Three of these earliest American tales are concerned with the effects of the Civil War on the love affairs of young Americans and contain the earliest versions, simplified but still apparent, of three future characters—Daisy Miller, Milly Theale, and the devoted, elderly widow so often found in James's fiction. There are three tales concerned with supernatural situations. Two tales present the peculiar problems of the artist, and one portrays an American female with characteristics—virtues and weaknesses—similar to those of Isabel Archer in *The Portrait of a Lady* and a blunt American male similar to Christopher Newman in *The American*.

Such classification cannot be precise, yet even such a brief statement about these early tales indicates that at the start of his career James is occupied with certain themes and characters he is to use again, with many variations, in his tales and novels. Already in these first eleven tales a reader finds the supernatural, the frustrated love affair, the predicament of the artist, American females—frivolous *and* serious in character—and the ambitious, seemingly blunt American male. The Civil War, which plays an important part in certain of these early tales, is a subject that appears occasionally throughout his work but is never again a major concern.

During the years he was writing these earliest tales, James lived mostly in Boston and Cambridge, Massachusetts. They were both exciting and painful years for him, or at least he looked back on them as filled with conflict.[3] On the one side there was pleasure and satisfaction. He was living well at home and meeting many of the literary men of Boston and New York. He visited acquaintances in Newport and the White Mountains, and he admired and perhaps loved his cousin, Minny Temple. He had good friends in Thomas Sergeant Perry, John La Farge, and Oliver Wendell Holmes. Yet there was the other, painful side. He saw his country at war, although he was not fit to fight, or considered himself unfit because he was in serious pain from a back injury, his "obscure hurt." [4] He was not happy at home, since he was uncertain of his career and realized that he must choose a direction. He made furtive attempts at writing.[5] He was given professional assistance and encouragement, but he found American society in general only slightly responsive to his quiet nature; at least most American society was not interesting to him. Would he be able in such an environment to justify his life as an artist and pay his way; or would he always feel insignificant facing the active force of men like Holmes, who represented the dynamic qualities America seemed more to admire? [6]

This period ended for James in February, 1869, when he left for his first trip as an adult to Europe. He stayed for fifteen months. When he returned to the United States in 1870, he had chosen his direction. As he wrote to Charles Eliot Norton in 1871, he felt his work as a writer was before him; such a creative task was to be demanding for an American because the quality of American life lay hidden beneath its plain surface:

> Looking about for myself, I conclude that the face of nature and civilization in this our country is to a certain point a very sufficient literary field. But it will yield its secrets only to a really *grasping* imagination. . . . To write well and worthily of American things one need even more than elsewhere to be a *master*. But unfortunately one is less! [7]

The tone here is resigned but not completely, nor was James completely serious. He saw a possible subject in American society, but at this point he did not clearly see his way to that subject. The way was—odd as it no doubt seemed to him and to others—to leave America and in his evolving international condition to see America in relation to established European civilizations. In this way America yielded its secrets to his grasping imagination. Such a way demanded time and experimentation, and before he wrote his best international tales and accepted his residence abroad, James created a series of early, exploratory tales of American society. These act as the foundation of his future fiction.

The most successful of the first eleven tales by James are "A Landscape Painter" (1866), "A Day of Days" (1866), "Poor Richard" (1867), "The Story of a Masterpiece" (1868), and "A Most Extraordinary Case" (1868).⁸ In this group are two of the three Civil War tales, the two tales about artists, and the one with a woman similar to Isabel Archer and a man like Christopher Newman. These are the most satisfactory tales because they are written with the greatest stylistic control and contain the most fully conceived characters and situations.

Each is interesting for another reason as well. Near the beginning of the first volume of his autobiography, *A Small Boy and Others*, James comments on a period in America earlier than the one during which these tales were written, but a similar period of exciting and disturbing youthful discovery. This comment, made in his late style as he looked back over the long road of his life, naturally shows an awareness of his purpose greater than he had as a young writer, but these earliest tales convey in particular the attitude of this late and reflective comment:

> It is for some record of the question of taste, of the consciousness of an aesthetic appeal, as reflected in forms and aspects, that I shall like best to testify; as the promise and the development of these things on our earlier American scene are the more interesting to trace for their doubtless demanding a degree of the finer attention. The plain and happy profusions and advances and successes, as one looks back, reflect themselves at every turn; the quick beats of the material increase and multiplication, with plenty of people to tell of them and throw up their caps for them; but the edifying matters to recapture would be the adventures of the "higher criticism" so far as there was any—and so far too as it might bear on the real quality and virtue of things; the state of manners, the terms of intercourse, the care for excellence, the sense of appearances, the intellectual reaction generally.⁹

It is precisely as "higher criticism" of life in America —the diverse manners, the style of intercourse, the intellectual tone—rather than of its material advances and successes, that the best of the early stories can still be read. Certainly they are not as good as some later tales or novels—then James had the European contrast to sharpen his insight—but they are a special form of criticism of the strictly American social scene—what amounts for James to a "picture" of what the private life of intelligent and sensitive Americans was like at this time. James is concerned in these tales with what we most often understand as "social" history. He does not discuss the actual events of the Civil War, but what the war means to the people who live through it; not how people make their money, but how they live with it; not the places they live in or go to visit, but the way they affect one another in these places. Even as early as 1865 when his second tale—"The Story of a Year"—was published, he knew what direction he wanted his fiction to take:

> I have no intention of following Lieutenant Ford to the seat of war. The exploits of his campaign are recorded in the public journals of the day, where the curious may still peruse them. My own taste has always been for unwritten history, and my present business is with the reverse of the picture. (I, 62)

"Poor Richard" (1867) shows "the reverse of the picture." It is not a completely successful tale, since James is uncertain of his direction, but it is an interesting one because it reveals his personal attitude about America and shows him developing certain important themes and characters. A young man, Richard Maule, does not go to fight in the Civil War but remains at home, just as James did.[10] Richard is in love with a wealthy young lady, Gertrude Whittaker, who sees him as a foolish, headstrong boy too romantic for a world that is so torn by war. She feels a kinship and responsibility for him, as he has lost his parents just as she has, but he is too weak for her to love. She falls in love with Captain Severn, a Civil War officer, but Richard in his jealousy is able to withhold information that confuses and ends this affair. He himself does not succeed, but rather his accomplice and fellow suitor, Major Luttrel. A ruthless and shrewd man exactly suited to this brutal world, Luttrel is able to give Gertrude the protection she needs. After a long illness and just before her marriage, Richard reveals to Gertrude what he and Luttrel have done, and she breaks the engagement to the major. Richard goes to war, returns a more sober man, and plans, once he has money, to go West to start again. Gertrude, equally unable to live in her society, sells her land and settles alone in Florence, protected by her money from the life she wants but cannot accept. Only Luttrel succeeds in his desires and marries a Philadelphia girl and her "seventy thousand a year."

James tells the story with simplicity and directness, yet without limiting the complexity of the emotions. Richard is not just a pathetic liar and a drunkard who wastes his fortune. He is even a potentially decent human being, and the problem for him is genuine: he fights against being the kind of man he believes such a brutal world requires. Gertrude at moments wants him to grow into a man she could love, but "she found herself weaker than he, while the happiness of both of them demanded that she should be stronger" (I, 195). In order to be free to love, she must be protected by someone from the world's harsh demands.

Captain Severn, the man Gertrude loves, is not a paragon, but rather a simple, decent man, "apparently quite contented with his lot" (I, 205). He is killed in battle not because he is weak like Richard, but because he does not retreat from the reality of his destructive world. Gertrude loves him for herself, but she hopes his natural, male presence will help Richard to be less occupied with his reflection and self-pity. There is even a suggestion that she hopes Severn will help to make Richard man enough to be someone she could marry.

It is difficult to understand exactly what Gertrude is meant to express, since James is uncertain in developing her character. A reader is confused as to what motivates her, what stops her from acting, apart from an ill-defined sensitivity, a vague sense of decency, an uncertain fear of the world's harshness. One might say as much for Milly Theale in *The Wings of the Dove*, but in that work James makes us see Milly by creating dramatic and expressive situations. Milly is meant to be James's tribute to the ineradicable impression of Minny Temple, as, in part, is Isabel Archer in *The Portrait of a Lady*. Minny, a cousin who died in 1870, was James's first "love," but how serious is uncertain. What is certain is that she represented an ideal American woman for James, a woman of courage and character. Gertrude Whittaker is *not* Minny Temple—she has a negativism that Minny seems never to have shown—but she does suggest certain qualities similar to Minny's, and Minny was the woman around whom revolved James, Oliver Wendell Holmes, and John Chipman Gray during their 1865 vacation that probably served as a source for the tale.[11] Between the writing of "Poor Richard" in 1867 and *The Wings of the Dove* in 1902, James grew as an artist. The uncertainty he has about Gertrude's character that he frankly states in the tale is what he is able to overcome in creating Milly Theale: "The truth is that Gertrude's private and personal emotions were entertained in a chamber of her heart so remote from the portals of speech that no sound of their revelry found its way into the world" (I, 207). Nor do these emotions clearly find their way into the tale; they are only suggested.

Gertrude is James's first attempt to create that unique American woman of intellectual grace, moral sensitivity, and great courage that no corruption could touch, but whose commitment to life could be destroyed by a harsh and deceitful world. Three years after writing "Poor Richard," in a letter to his brother, William James, Henry is able to state more clearly what he is seeking in creating Gertrude. He makes this comment as he contrasts the Americans and the English: "I revolt from their [the English women's] dreary deathly want of—what shall I call it?—Clover Hooper has it—intellectual grace—Minny Temple has it—moral spontaneity." [12] What is interesting about his comment is not only what he finds exceptional in Minny Temple that one finds suggested in Gertrude and created in Milly Theale, but that as he moves toward his international contrasts, he comes *closer* to the definition of certain American virtues that previously, as in his creation of Gertrude, he only vaguely understood. It is in going abroad that he gains the perspective to understand the America he left.

It is possible then to see the tale as representing James's personal and distant relationship to the war and to certain friends. Richard perhaps reflects James's own insecurity at this period and his uncertainty about what he would do with his fondness for feeling and thinking in a world that appears so slightly concerned with these reflective matters. More than a personal comment, the tale presents "higher criticism" of a society affected by war; depicts in Richard the image of the destroyed youth; and reveals in his relation to Gertrude the cracks in the civilization, in the homes and private affairs many miles from the battle lines. As a picture of society the tale is suggestive enough to be of considerable interest, even though James is attempting in Gertrude a portrait of an American woman that it will take many years and much experience with Europe to bring into sharp focus.

That this tale is simply and directly written helps to explain its limited success. James does not always write his early tales so simply. He often removes himself, telling his story through a first-person narrator, a letter-writer, a diarist.[13] The first-person narrator *sometimes* needlessly complicates a tale by introducing an unnecessary character who does not contribute to the story, although such a narrator does give another point of view that can effectively contribute to the tale's psychological interest. In James's early tales the use of the first-person narrator often comes with, or perhaps produces, a somewhat detached, humorous, and superior tone of voice that further confuses the impact of the story. "Poor Richard" is written without any intruding elements, and its directness creates greater control and effect.

Perhaps the most important aspect of the tale is its tentative concern with a significant Jamesian theme. The theme is not fully expressed in this tale, and it is necessary to refer to other of James's works to make clear his intention. At one point in the story Gertrude says to herself about her love for Captain Severn and her desire to live her life for him, " 'If you won't risk anything how can you demand of others that they shall?' " (I, 219). She is asking how much of herself she is willing to risk to live the life she wants. For a James character to "live" life is neither easy to do, nor easy to see how to do. The process as it is portrayed in James's fiction has to do with observing, experiencing, risking, taking a chance that might demand a sacrifice. The terms are given here in the progression of what is personally demanded. One builds experience on observation, risks on experience, sacrifices on risks taken, and at each point is aware of what one is doing. Gertrude's comment to herself comes at the end of a long paragraph of self-examination in which she admits that she cannot act the fool, as Richard acts about her, and show her love to Captain Severn. She maintains she is too much her father's proper daughter: " 'I love that man, but I love myself better' "

(I, 219). In effect, she refuses to risk her pride for love in order to have the life she wants. In the end both she and Richard must sacrifice, not for what they want but for what they have lost.[14]

This "life" that they seek is not explicit in "Poor Richard," perhaps because it is always difficult to say exactly what life is, perhaps because the young writer is uncertain of himself and of his characters. What James means by "life" is, however, fundamental to an understanding of his early tales.[15] If one does not have some sense of what he means by this word, his stories will not be coherent.

James's comment made in 1874 in an article on Turgenev will help us to understand this broad term.

> Life *is*, in fact, a battle. On this point optimists and pessimists agree. Evil is insolent and strong; beauty enchanting but rare; goodness very apt to be weak; folly very apt to be defiant; wickedness to carry the day; imbeciles to be in great places, people of sense in small, and mankind generally, unhappy. But the world as it stands is no illusion, no phantasm, no evil dream of a night; we wake up to it again for ever and ever; we can neither forget it nor deny it nor dispense with it. We can welcome experience as it comes, and give it what it demands, in exchange for something which it is idle to pause to call much or little so long as it contributes to swell the volume of consciousness. In this there is mingled pain and delight, but over the mysterious mixture there hovers a visible rule, that bids us learn to will and seek to understand.[16]

This is an unusual recognition of what life is for the young Henry James. Seeing such a life, experiencing it, taking risks, making sacrifices for what one desires, is a delicate, difficult process. Such a life has a Medusa face, as James himself said; it can make apparent evil into good and seeming good into evil. It can create strength in weakness, weakness in apparent strength. Richard and

Gertrude fail to accept the conflicting demands of such a world and give in: they do not accept the invisible rule "that bids us learn to will and seek to understand." Although their failure is, in part, imposed by a cruel world, it is still a personal failure, for the world is always cruel. The Civil War is only a symbol for the harsh reality they must contend with. They try to forget, to deny, the truth of this world as it is; but reality intrudes, as it must. At the end of the tale they are resigned to accepting what has happened and will happen to them, but they have no realization of what "living" life demands. They are not committed; they seem to have lived all the life they will ever have. James even suggests, at the end of the tale, that Gertrude might accept Richard, but now he no longer can see what he has always wanted to see.

Several of the other early tales are also concerned with the question of how much to risk in love in order to take fully from life. One of the most interesting of these is "A Day of Days" (1866), a short tale written when James was just twenty-three. Thomas Ludlow—"a certain crudity of manner and aspect proved him to belong to the great vulgar, muscular, popular majority" (I, 144)—arrives in the country on a fine September morning to visit Herbert Moore, a fellow scientist. Ludlow is to sail the next day for Europe. Mr. Moore is not at home, but his sister, Adela, greets Ludlow. She is a woman of sophistication and character who has left the world of fashion because she feared it was making her a shallow person who might, as she comments about a friend, talk "about her lover with almost indecent flippancy" (I, 141). On this day, however, she is alone and half regretting her decision, wondering what will happen to her in the future, wishing for more of life than the local Unitarian minister can offer. Ludlow procrastinates in hopes of at least a pleasant day in the country with the sister, if not a talk with the brother who might return in the meantime. They have that day, and it is so perfect that Ludlow is willing to miss his boat on the chance of their falling in love; but Adela must, he says, ask that he remain. She cannot, and he leaves in time to catch the boat.

That is not all the story. James implies that Ludlow would have missed his boat "for sufficient cause—at the suggestion of a fact" (I, 164), but he is not given the fact and so does not take the risk. That he does not seems Adela's fault, as Ludlow is waiting for her to speak; but that he must have a fact is clearly his own weakness. For James, an insistence on "facts" often makes life less exciting, and can even make reality false —witness Strether's pursuit of the facts in *The Ambassadors*. Strether only grasps reality when he lets go of the facts around which he had previously structured his life. Certainly Ludlow's insistence on facts makes for less than he wants. If he had wanted Adela, perhaps he should have accepted the risk without any assurance, or at least realized that for her a direct statement was as hard to give as it was for him to act without such concreteness.

This concept of "facts" seems to extend the story beyond what James considered at the time of writing. There is little evidence for such an interpretation, except as we can refine the story in light of the later James. Ludlow, who is much like Christopher Newman with his brash, common but honest manner, going as he is to Europe for culture, is meant to be a choice Adela cannot face because she cannot risk enough for the raw but real life he presents. Shortly after she meets him, she becomes conscious of his natural vibrancy. "The morning light covered his face, and, mingled with that of his radiant laugh, showed Adela that his was a nature very much alive" (I, 147). By habit and convention she is too much concerned with questions of form and manners

that are, when it comes to Ludlow's uncommon character, irrelevant and superficial. She is as flippant as her
friend, and her retreat to the country has not saved her.
Adela continues after the above comment to say to herself:

> "Whatever else he may be . . . I think he is honest. I am
> afraid he isn't a gentleman—but he isn't a bore." She met
> his eye, freely, for a moment. "What do you want of my
> benevolence?" she asked, with an abruptness of which she
> was perfectly conscious. "Does he wish to make friends,"
> she pursued tacitly, "or does he merely wish to pay me a
> vulgar compliment? There is bad taste, perhaps, in either
> case, but especially in the latter." (I, 147)

She does suggest to him that he not leave at once, but it
is *her* final refusal to risk the possibility of something
more that limits their encounter to the single incident.

Adela is a woman too sophisticated for common pleas-
ures, but not wise enough to see that her sophistication
is restrictive. Like Isabel Archer in *The Portrait of a
Lady*, although without Isabel's complexity, Adela is the
American woman of quality and sensitivity with a tragic
blind spot when it comes to seeing what will give her the
life she wants. Ludlow, like Isabel's suitor, Caspar Goodwood, does go beyond certain limits of taste and reserve,
but unlike Isabel's American, Ludlow has the reader's
sympathy. He is not the choice that will make for less—
as it seems Goodwood is—but the choice that is too
much for Adela. In the end she retreats into the safe
position for a correct lady, losing whatever freedom and
life this "day of days" might have given her.

It is important to read the story against the setting of
contemporary nineteenth-century social behavior. Adela,
in allowing herself to see and talk to Ludlow, has clearly
gambled for more than is proper for a young lady. She is
driven to do so by the beautiful day, her loneliness, and
her concern that she is twenty-five and must consider her

future. James says that "she had pretty well unlearned her old dignities and forms, but she was to break with them still more completely" (I, 162). She does ignore certain of the restrictions of her background and nature, but she is not free enough to act as she really wants. The whole question of the forms proper to a lady, and to a gentleman, establishes the framework of the tale. Without these forms of the American nineteenth-century society, subjected to James's criticism, there would be none of the beauty and frustration that are found in this unusual encounter. James is not judging right and wrong so much as commenting on the freedom of movement permitted against such a social background. It is this American world that the young James himself found so confining because it so limited the area of significant and valid response. Adela is the symbol of the failure even the best of such a world must suffer when it confronts "life," since that world's conception of life is so rigid and incomplete. Adela is a too-simply-stated character, as James will know by the time he creates the more absorbing but similar Isabel Archer; the complexity in Isabel's character will be achieved then not alone in his better understanding of the American woman, but also in the contrast of her with the more various social scene of Europe.

It is easy to slight Ludlow, since it is easy to imagine him only as an early version of Christopher Newman, somewhat more bookish but still little more than the forward, blunt, culture-seeking American. The similarity is there, but Ludlow is a refinement on the American, one that James does not further develop in his novels, or at least not as fully as he might. James's initial description of Ludlow shows how he resembles Newman, but also differs from him.

A certain crudity of manner and aspect proved him to belong to the great vulgar, muscular, popular majority. On this basis, however, he was a sufficiently good-looking fellow: a middle-sized, agile figure, a head so well shaped as to be handsome, a pair of inquisitive, responsive eyes, and a large manly mouth, constituting the most expressive part of his equipment. Turned upon the world at an early age, he had, in the pursuit of a subsistence, tried his head at everything in succession, and had generally found it to be quite as hard as the opposing substance; and his person may have been thought to reflect this experience in an air of taking success too much for granted. He was a man of strong faculties and a strong will, but it is doubtful whether his feelings were stronger than he. People liked him for his directness, his good-humour, his general soundness and serviceableness, and disliked him for the same qualities under different names; that is, for his impudence, his offensive optimism, his inhuman avidity for facts. When his friends insisted upon his noble disinterestedness, his enemies were wont to reply it was all very well to ignore, to suppress, one's own sensibilities in the pursuit of knowledge, but to trample on the rest of mankind at the same time betrayed an excess of zeal. Fortunately for Ludlow, on the whole, he was no great listener, and even if he had been, a certain plebeian thick-skinnedness would always have saved his tenderer parts; although it must be added that, if, like a genuine democrat, he was very insensitive, like a genuine democrat, too, he was unexpectedly proud. (I, 144–45)

The difference between Ludlow and Newman is slight but significant. In the balance, Ludlow seems to come out with more of the reader's respect. As the best product of the vulgar majority, he is unusually good. Of course, so is Newman; but James creates the feeling that no matter how right Newman is, the Bellegardes are not more right, perhaps, but more aware. It is they who make Newman act as he does. Ludlow is clearly—as stated in the comparison made earlier to Caspar Goodwood and as appears in the above description of him—common, decent, and *not* a choice that makes for less, but possibly a choice that makes for much more. James could have developed his central characters on the level of Ludlow, but he chose first to develop his main characters on what seems a lesser level, into Christopher Newman and Daisy Miller. However, even this type of American becomes uninteresting to him and soon appears in his fiction as very common indeed, even as a slightly unpleasant minor character like Henrietta Stackpole, or like Caspar Goodwood.

James goes in another direction from Ludlow or Newman and Daisy. He drops the Americans of the vulgar masses for the special and uncommon Americans, such as Isabel Archer, Milly Theale, Maggie Verver, and Lambert Strether. James seems to need their fine consciousness to hold his own and to find little interest in the "unusual common" type that Ludlow represents. It could be said that the civilizing virtues of democracy interest James less than its civilized ideal. In his longer fiction, it is only Francie Dosson, the heroine of *The Reverberator*, who successfully suggests a complexity of character in the same way as Ludlow. She is the common woman with distinct qualities, a Daisy Miller, admittedly, but one with the saving grace of an unusual sense of her personal dignity. She finally marries the Frenchman on her own terms and really because she is so exceptionally willing to lose him unless he accepts her just as she is. And the reader is clearly meant to admire her, and the Frenchman for his decision to marry her.

Of the three remaining early tales that are particularly interesting, two can be briefly discussed, since their contribution to James's development of themes is slight, and whatever significance they have in this area is better illustrated by other tales. "A Landscape Painter" (1866) is James's third tale and his earliest one about an artist— a tale he considered successful enough to republish.[17] The artistic theme is not essential to this tale as it will be to later ones. A rich young man and amateur painter, jilted in love by a society woman, marries a poor but proper New England girl, out of sympathy and love for her innocence, and finds that she has shrewdly married him with her eyes open. The denouement is contrived, and James awkwardly uses the device of a diary to tell the story. There are some effectively written and witty passages between the two lovers, particularly one long speech by the heroine in which she shows her incisive mind and the hero's limitations (I, 118–19). James suggests here the power latent in her, her determination to rise above her condition, which prepares the reader for the final action of her strong nature—she is capable of tricking her too blasé lover into marriage when it is he who has thought he was deceiving her. There is a fine section that describes in a painterly way a summer outing in a boat and a lunch on an island; James allows the pleasant freedom of the experience to be expressed in delightfully easy dialogue. The tale also shows how early James begins to concentrate upon the psychological study of two people in love who play with appearance and reality to achieve their purpose—a theme he will return to again, and more effectively, in later tales.

"A Most Extraordinary Case" (1868) is a Civil War tale, also republished by James. In it a wounded hero falls in love with a vibrant young woman and silently fails to recover his will to live because she loves another man, his doctor. Ferdinand Mason, the wounded hero, believes he wants to live, but never realizes he has not learned how. All his life has been spent in keeping busy. His illness is not just caused by his wound, but is an exhaustion resulting from never having experienced anything in life that would now prepare him to live deeply: once he loves and loses he is not capable of recovering. James perceptively sees war as that which accentuates the human condition, releasing our weaknesses in "wounds." That Mason wants to live and that circumstances of love stop him give the tale certain similarities to *The Wings of the Dove*; in his physical and emotional condition, the wounded soldier also prefigures Ralph Touchett of *The Portrait of a Lady*. The tale is effectively written, and James gives the reader a delicate insight into the character of the dying soldier. There is an elderly, good-natured American matron in the story who acts as a fairy godmother. This character is a type James uses again, most often as one of the means to set the events of his novels and tales in motion and keep them going, as do Mrs. Touchett in *The Portrait of a Lady* and Mrs. Stringham in *The Wings of the Dove*.

William James, writing to Henry soon after the appearance of this tale, made an important observation, one that applies to James's fiction in general:

> I am just in from the theatre and feel like dropping you a line to tell you I have got your last *Atlantic* story ("Extraordinary Case"), and read it with much satisfaction. It makes me think I may have partly misunderstood your aim heretofore, and that one of the objects you have had in view has been to give an impression like that we often get of people in life: Their orbits come out of space and lay themselves for a short time along of ours, and then off they whirl again into the unknown, leaving us with little more than an impression of their reality and a feeling of baffled curiosity as to the mystery of the beginning and end of their being, and of the intimate character of that segment of it which we have seen. Am I right in guessing that you had a conscious intention of this sort here? . . . You seem to acknowledge that you can't exhaust any character's feelings or thoughts by an articulate displaying of them. You shrink from the attempt to drag them all reeking and dripping and raw upon the stage, which most writers make and fail in. You expressly restrict yourself, accordingly, to showing a few external acts and speeches, and by the magic of your art making the reader *feel* back of these the existence of a body of being of which these

are casual features. You wish to suggest a mysterious
fulness which you do not lead the reader through. It
seems to me this is a very legitimate method, and has a
great effect when it succeeds. . . . Only it must succeed.[18]

That James did have this attitude and that most of what
he wrote is based upon it is generally accepted. For many
readers *The Portrait of a Lady* seems to stop abruptly
and inconclusively. James knew that his readers would
think this and commented in one of his notebooks:
"The obvious criticism of course will be that it is not
finished—that I have not seen the heroine to the end of
her situation—that I have left her *en l'air*.—This is both
true and false. The *whole* of anything is never told; you
can only take what groups together. What I have done
has that unity—it groups together. It is complete in itself
—and the rest may be taken up or not, later." [19] The
point is perhaps less obvious in reading the early tales
where it might seem that they are inconclusive, not
because James wanted them to be, but because they do
not contain the material necessary for our understanding. In certain tales this is true, but generally it is not.
William James's point is correct, and one is better able
to understand the early tales once it is accepted. Also,
once it is understood in reading other works of James, a
reader can move away from a surface concern with a
neatly patterned narrative to James's deeper concern
with a more complex view of life. James said in the
Preface to *Roderick Hudson*: "Really, universally, relations stop nowhere, and the exquisite problem of the
artist is eternally but to draw, by a geometry of his own,
the circle within which they shall happily *appear* to do
so." [20] "A Most Extraordinary Case," "Poor Richard,"
"A Day of Days," "A Landscape Painter"—all are conceived as "impressions" of the baffling mystery that William James discusses, as is so much of James's finest
fiction.

None of the tales of the supernatural—"The Romance

of Certain Old Clothes" (1868), "A Problem" (1868), "De Grey: A Romance" (1868)—is worth attention, since James begins by handling this genre too simply and sensationally. These are attempts to write Hawthorne-like tales of the supernatural before James saw how he could make this kind of tale psychologically unusual. "The Romance of Certain Old Clothes," a tale of a curse on clothes, is smoothly written, but its effect—the mysterious death of the heroine as she opens the chest of clothes—is so contrived and slight, and so long in coming, that the ending has not the shock it should have. The tale was reprinted twice by James. Later in life, in 1914, he strongly objected to its inclusion in an anthology, as he felt he had done better work.[21] "A Problem" is one of James's oddest and most banal tales: a couple are told by three different fortunetellers that their child will die and they will marry twice. They begin to argue and then separate, the child dies, and they reunite, hence fulfilling the prophecies. The tale, very flatly written, seems to have no other purpose than to prove that fortunetellers can be right, although not exactly as we think. "De Grey," the best written of these three, is based on a story by Balzac and has a strong old-world flavor, although its locale is America. One of the characters is the family Roman Catholic priest; the hero returns from Europe, his fiancée having died there, to live out an ancient family curse. It is the last written of the tales of this group and already shows the transition James will gradually make to his European-centered tales. Edel finds what he calls the "usurpation" theme in "De Grey" and "The Romance of Certain Old Clothes":

> We have situations involving a reversal of role between two persons closely linked and the supplanting of one by another: the older sister ["The Romance"] becomes the wife of her dead sister's husband and dies herself when she

would wear her sister's clothes. De Grey's bride becomes a vampire-like destroyer of the man destined to be her husband in order to save herself.[22]

The worst faults of these, and all the poorer early tales, are their frequent romantic or melodramatic situations which are often ludicrous, and their unintentionally humorous or mock-sophisticated tone, as if James were not confident enough of what he wanted to say to be serious. How these faults are mixed with certain qualities can be illustrated by "My Friend Bingham" (1867). The tale is far too contrived and melodramatic—a widow's son is accidentally shot by the hero and then he and the widow fall in love and marry—but the tale is delicately written in many places and contains two main characters who are, in spite of the melodrama of their situation, sensitively conceived, showing James's growing ability to portray complex characters. There is an interesting opening paragraph in which the young writer betrays his early fascination with the mixture of life's bitter-sweet quality, what he refers to later as a "strange . . . alloy," in his Preface to *What Maisie Knew*. This opening paragraph illustrates how James's tone becomes unintentionally humorous as he attempts a false sophistication. The paragraph also shows how James uses the superfluous narrator, once removed from the central action, to get into the story.

> Conscious as I am of a deep aversion to stories of a painful nature, I have often asked myself whether, in the events here set forth, the element of pain is stronger than that of joy. An affirmative answer to this question would have stood as a veto upon the publication of my story, for it is my opinion that the literature of horrors needs no extension. Such an answer, however, I am unwilling to pronounce; while, on the other hand, I hesitate to assume the responsibility of a decided negative. I have therefore determined to leave the solution to the reader. I may add,

that I am very sensible of the superficial manner in which
I have handled my facts. I bore no other part in the
accomplishment of these facts than that of a cordial
observer; and it was impossible that, even with the best
will in the world, I should fathom the emotions of the
actors. Yet, as the very faintest reflection of human passions, under the pressure of fate, possesses an immortal
interest, I am content to appeal to the reader's sympathy,
and to assure him of my own fidelity. (I, 165)

"The Story of a Year" (1865) presents the earliest
version of the Daisy Miller type in the shallow Elizabeth
("Lizzie") Crowe, although her intellect and conscience
are far more limited than Daisy's. As Miss Kelley points
out, the end of this tale—the death of the hero—is an
evasion, not a solution, and James's style is too frequently flowery to be satisfactory.[23] Krishna Baldev Vaid
sees in this tale the mock-serious tone mentioned above.

One reason for this garrulous bonhomie may be that
James is dealing here with a more complex situation and
does not yet have the requisite mastery over his material;
consequently he seeks to slur over some of the difficult
moments by a rather naive admission of his inability to
render them.[24]

Edel makes an interesting comment on the trio of characters in "The Story of a Year"—mother, ward, and son:

The three figures in the foreground were to reappear in
many forms in James's later fiction—the determined
mother, her ward or protégé or relative, and the young son
in love, unsure of himself, fearing to assert himself, and if
he does, paying for it by personal disintegration. Mrs.
Ford is a somewhat fiercer Mrs. Garland, John Ford an
ineffectual and inartistic Roderick and Elizabeth a shallow Mary Garland. The situation recurs with quite other
types in The Portrait of a Lady—Mrs. Touchett, Isabel
and Ralph.[25]

Admittedly this tale has its Jamesian qualities. The description of scenery and events is used to suggest the emotion of a character or the interaction of two characters, at times effectively, at times too dramatically; Lizzie Crowe's shallow nature is sketched with a lightness that shows an unusually certain insight for one so young as James. Yet the focus of the tale is not clear. James begins the tale by suggesting a parallel between the son going to the Civil War, perhaps to be killed in battle—as indeed he is—and his being "killed" at home in the battle for his soul, fought by his mother and her ward; but James loses this focus that relates society to the individual as he develops in Lizzie the hollow, beautiful, and unconsciously destructive American girl. It is as if James could not avoid this fascinating American female and shows himself here, at the start of his career, more a psychological than a sociological writer.

There is one final tale in this early group that can serve as a summary of the ideas that have been so far discussed. "The Story of a Masterpiece" (1868) is not usually considered one of James's better tales, but it is a deceptive story. On first reading, it seems too brittle in style. It moves too quickly and has a detached, slightly mock-humorous tone. On further readings, the shallowness of the style and the flippancy of tone appear to be intentional. James uses these satirical techniques to reinforce his criticism of the characters who represent this shallowness and speak in such a voice. One can be misled by the highly polished veneer of this tale and fail to respond to the "higher criticism" of American society that is being made. Although the tale does not state moral judgments, it clearly implies them as it exposes through the style and tone of voice the artificiality and conventionality of the two main characters. The most complete vision of reality in the tale comes through a portrait, a masterpiece, by a young American painter. Art

becomes the subtlest expression of the complex, bitter-
sweet quality that is life. In the end the masterpiece is
destroyed: one character tries to deny the vision art has
given him; the other never sees the vision of art. The tale
does not conclude but ends with the events of the future
uncertain: "How he has fared—how he is destined to
fare . . . it is rather too early to determine" (I, 296).[26]

John Lennox, a wealthy widower in his mid-thirties, is
soon to marry a lady younger than he, of small means
but of great beauty—Marian Everett. He is very much in
love and believes that in his marriage he will find an
ideal happiness. He arranges for a young artist, Stephen
Baxter, to paint his fiancée's portrait as a wedding present. Marian sees the finished work as flattering to her,
but Lennox soon realizes that Baxter has brutally expressed the soul of his fiancée while still portraying her
beauty. In the portrait she appears to Lennox as a heart-
less woman. It is revealed that Baxter had once loved
Marian, and she had deceived him as she had other men.
Lennox suspects the first and does not know the second,
but realizes that Baxter in his portrait has captured the
real character of his fiancée, something Lennox could
not see because of his narrow vision, just as Baxter could
not while he was in love. Lennox debates whether or not
he should marry, for he believes Baxter is right in his
portrayal, but finally he decides to go through with it.
The night before the wedding he slashes the portrait and
accepts his wife as a woman he knows is shallow and
miserably lacking in any of the profound qualities he had
hoped for. Of course, Marian knows nothing, either of
what he thinks or what she is, and Baxter says nothing.

The mockery, the cynical detachment of observation,
the implied critique of manners and characters, appear
at once. Pointed to, these elements seem obvious, but
they have not been generally noted. Here as an example
of the style and tone are the first several paragraphs of

the tale. They are quoted completely and consecutively to give an indication of James's method.

No longer ago than last summer, during a six weeks' stay at Newport, John Lennox became engaged to Miss Marian Everett of New York. Mr Lennox was a widower, of large estate, and without children. He was thirty-five years old, of a sufficiently distinguished appearance, of excellent manners, of an unusual share of sound information, of irreproachable habits and of a temper which was understood to have suffered a trying and salutary probation during the short term of his wedded life. Miss Everett was, therefore, all things considered, believed to be making a very good match and to be having by no means the worst of the bargain.

And yet Miss Everett, too, was a very marriageable young lady—the pretty Miss Everett, as she was called, to distinguish her from certain plain cousins, with whom, owing to her having no mother and no sisters, she was constrained, for decency's sake, to spend a great deal of her time—rather to her own satisfaction, it may be conjectured, than to that of these excellent young women.

Marian Everett was penniless, indeed; but she was richly endowed with all the gifts which make a woman charming. She was, without dispute, the most charming girl in the circle in which she lived and moved. Even certain of her elders, women of a larger experience, of a heavier calibre, as it were, and, thanks to their being married ladies, of greater freedom of action, were practically not so charming as she. And yet, in her emulation of the social graces of these, her more fully licensed sisters, Miss Everett was quite guiltless of any aberration from the strict line of maidenly dignity. She professed an almost religious devotion to good taste, and she looked with horror upon the boisterous graces of many of her companions. Beside being the most entertaining girl in New York, she was, therefore, also the most irreproachable. Her beauty was, perhaps, contestable, but it was certainly uncontested. She was the least bit below middle height, and her person was marked by a great fullness and roundness of outline; and yet, in spite of this comely ponderosity, her movements were perfectly light and elastic. In complexion, she was genuine blonde—a warm blonde; with a midsummer bloom upon her cheek, and the light of a midsummer sun wrought into her auburn hair. Her features were not cast upon a classical model, but their expression was in the highest degree pleasing. Her forehead was low and broad, her nose small, and her mouth— well, by the envious her mouth was called *enormous*. It is certain that it had an immense capacity for smiles, and that when she opened it to sing (which she did with infinite sweetness) it emitted a copious flood of sound. Her face was, perhaps, a trifle too circular, and her shoulders a trifle too high; but, as I say, the general effect left nothing to be desired. I might point out a dozen discords in the character of her face and figure, and yet utterly fail to invalidate the impression they produced. There is something essentially uncivil, and, indeed, unphilosophical, in the attempt to verify or to disprove a woman's beauty in detail, and a man gets no more than he deserves when he finds that, in strictness, the aggregation of the different features fails to make up the total. Stand off, gentlemen, and let *her* make the addition. Beside her beauty, Miss Everett shone by her good nature and her lively perceptions. She neither made harsh speeches nor resented them; and, on the other hand, she keenly enjoyed intellectual cleverness, and even cultivated it. Her great merit was that she made no claims or pretensions. Just as there was nothing artificial in her beauty, so there was nothing pedantic in her acuteness and nothing sentimental in her amiability. The one was all freshness and the others all *bonhomie*. (I, 259–60)

The writing here, depending on one's point of view and one's sense of humor, is either ironic, like Miss Everett's enormous mouth, or—as has often been thought in considering this tale—an immature failure in style and tone.[27] That Miss Everett emerges later in the tale as a hideous

combination of surface beauties that suggests her gro-
tesquely ill-shaped soul, and that Mr. Lennox appears an
immature, conventionally oriented young man, should
indicate how carefully James goes about his business at
the start. True, he is not serious here, and he expects us
to smile; but he is not being unintentionally light, and he
is being supremely critical. It is not until he introduces
his artist that he becomes "serious," but his satirical voice
and sharp observations at the start do not suggest that he
expects us to consider the situation as superficial. The
style, the tone, are only the surface—the bright brittle—
and below is what the artist will be serious about: two
supposedly intelligent people, representatives of society,
who, in fact, know very little because they are both
victims of forms. He deplores ignorance in "high" places;
these should be the places of intelligence and sensitivity.
In this tale, he locates these virtues in the lower, less
socially important positions of society. The difference
James establishes between the two is that those in high
places cannot observe because they cannot see anything
that does not fit their limiting forms, and those in lower
positions, free of such manneristic forms, are able to
observe all too well. They do not look upon the world
according to conventions.

To describe the artist Baxter as "low" is incorrect. He
is the classless artist, and he is clearly a more conscious
man than Lennox; but he is not, for all his inherent
quality, on the high social level of Lennox and Marian.
Democratically and correctly, James sees that Baxter is
fine because of what he inherently is: an observer who
makes his observations part of his life. Class has nothing
to do with his quality. He represents those who accept
what is seen, and as such he is the true aristocrat. Here,
as in the other tales examined in detail, James is attempting a descriptive critique of the limitations and restrictions of American society, but he is also moving toward

another idea. He is suggesting that one sees, interprets, reality to suit one's purpose and comfort. Marian shifts all reality to satisfy her vanity and hence sees little. Lennox sees more, but he does not want to accept the uncomfortable truth of what he sees. Only Baxter, the artist, is not duped. Baxter in his painting, like James in writing the story, must be disinterested and unmoved in his search for truth if he is to have the insight of an artist.

Justice must be done to Lennox, for he does suspect that his fiancée is not all he imagines her. He is a reserved, conventional man of limited experience who is overcome by an unexpected and too exciting romantic infatuation. The vision of Marian that Baxter confirms in the portrait, Lennox has suspected earlier. At one point in their engagement he asks, out of desperation at her blasé but still correct manner, " 'Marian, where *is* your heart?' " (I, 284). He is bothered by the too calculated, too easy shifts of her emotions in contrast to his all-possessing love. What he must be held responsible for is his failure to do anything with his observations. He is absurdly weak. Baxter comments to himself on this point.

> He had liked him and esteemed him; he had taken him for a man of sense and of feeling, and he had thought it a matter of regret that such a man—a creature of strong spiritual needs—should link his destiny with that of Marian Everett. But he had very soon made up his mind that Lennox knew very well what he was about, and that he needed no enlightenment. He was marrying with his eyes open, and had weighed the risks against the profits. Everyone had his particular taste, and at thirty-five years of age John Lennox had no need to be told that Miss Everett was not quite all that she might be. Baxter had thus taken for granted that his friend had designedly selected as his second wife a mere pretty woman—a woman with a gen-

ius for receiving company, and who would make a picturesque use of his money. He knew nothing of the serious
character of the poor man's passion, nor of the extent to
which his happiness was bound up in what the painter
would have called his delusion. (I, 286–87)

Lennox is childlike. His question to Marian is naïvely
unaware. If he doubts the existence of her heart, he
should not ask a question of this importance in such an
absurdly meaningless way. The problem is that his society has given him no means to deal with such a situation. He could not possibly expect more than he gets
from Marian when she answers his question by saying,
" 'Where—what do you mean?' " Lennox does not see
the cleverness in her superficial reply nor the unintentional truth, both of which should, even for his foolish
question, be answer enough. She later says, " 'My heart's
everywhere' " (I, 285), but even this remark does not
register with Lennox. Can Lennox, as Baxter wonders,
not realize that he is getting merely a "pretty" woman to
adorn his old age? Lennox sees, in part, what he is doing.
He sees as much as his experience allows him and after
much debate marries, "not for love, but for friendship,
and a little, perhaps, for prudence" (I, 292). Lennox
cannot, no matter how he tries, not have seen what he
has seen. He can only pretend he has not seen—which he
realizes is a further deception.

The incident of the portrait is the central one of the
tale; it should be remembered that this is the story of a
masterpiece. Actually the tale is concerned with two
portraits. When Lennox first comes to Baxter's studio he
sees Baxter's painting of Browning's poem, "My Last
Duchess," and finds that it slightly resembles Marian. It
is because of the resemblance, only partially intentional
as the portrait was started before Baxter knew Marian,
that Lennox begins to have his latent suspicions of Marian brought into focus. In one sense he asks himself if

she is not a type—the light woman, like the last duchess. "The Story of a Masterpiece" can be read as James's impression of the same multi-level view of reality that is in Browning's poem. What *is* reality in that poem? We might ask the same question at the end of James's story.[28]

At first glance it might appear that James accepts Browning's poem as merely an exposé of a superficial woman and that his tale is little more than another such exposé, regardless of its title. James's interpretation of this poem might be subtler, and so might our interpretation of his tale, if we look more closely at Marian. What we see in the tale depends on what we think of her. She is never accused of serious indiscretion, only of being the subject of great affection she cannot ignore, somewhat as Daisy Miller expects and accepts the love of all men. Her "affair" with Baxter is slightly more serious, particularly for him; but her main fault is that she is beautiful and desires to please, and she does so indiscriminately and with pleasure: "She had cared for nothing but pleasure; but to what else were girls brought up?" (I, 292). She is like Daisy Miller: a woman of beauty whose soul is not corrupt or corrupting, simply shallow and incomplete. Like Daisy she has her affair with Baxter while in Europe, accompanied not by a sick mother but by a sick companion. Unlike Daisy she does not catch fever wandering Rome at night, simply because she is too vain and conniving to be that naïve. It is never she who expects more of herself, but those who fall victim to her beauty and then are disappointed that she does not have the rich soul she never claimed to have. She is pleased when men like her and shrewd in her defense when they attack her. She is, in this sense, more as we imagine Browning's duchess to be—a beautiful woman, femininely clever, somewhat too easy, too indiscriminate, but not evil. In the profound sense she is shallow, annoyingly so, but it is never she who claims to be more than she is. Perhaps in Browning and James it is the superficial society that is most to blame, a society that sanctions her place and the men who desire her pleasure. If she were not allowed to succeed *only* because of her enormous beauty, she would never be given the chance to lead men on as she does.

Again, depending on one's point of view, the portrait Baxter paints of her is either brilliant or brutal. It is either one or both because it is true. It is its truth to life that Lennox, in his formalistic blindness, cannot stand. He is not prepared to live seeing life that closely. After the brief affair between Marian and Baxter, this comment is made at the end of the narrative of their adventure.

> The ample justice, moreover, which, under the illusion of sentiment, he had rendered to her charms and graces, gave him a right, when free from that illusion, to register his estimate of the arid spaces of her nature. Miss Everett might easily have accused him of injustice and brutality; but this fact would still stand to plead in his favor, that he cared with all his strength for truth. Marian, on the contrary, was quite indifferent to it. (I, 279)

Lennox when he sees Marian's portrait objects to it as being " 'too hard, too strong, of too frank a reality' " (I, 282), and Baxter answers that he goes " 'in for reality; you must have seen that.' " When Lennox looks at the finished portrait, he sees the reality he has suspected but would not admit until art forced him to do so.

> It seemed to Lennox that some strangely potent agency had won from his mistress the confession of her inmost soul, and had written it there upon the canvas in firm yet passionate lines. Marian's person was lightness—her charm was lightness; could it be that her soul was levity too? Was she a creature without faith and without conscience? What else was the meaning of that horrible blankness and deadness that quenched the light in her

eyes and stole away the smile from her lips? These things were the less to be eluded because in so many respects the painter had been profoundly just. He had been as loyal and sympathetic as he had been intelligent. Not a point in the young girl's appearance had been slighted; not a feature but had been forcibly and delicately rendered. Had Baxter been a man of marvellous insight—an unparalleled observer; or had he been a mere patient and unflinching painter, building infinitely better than he knew? Would not a mere painter have been content to paint Miss Everett in the strong, rich, objective manner of which the work was so good an example, and to do nothing more? For it was evident that Baxter had done more. He had painted with something more than knowledge—with imagination, with feeling. He had almost *composed*; and his composition had embraced the truth. Lennox was unable to satisfy his doubts. (I, 285)

This is the vision the artist has given to Lennox and to us. James comments that Baxter "had painted with something more than knowledge—with imagination, with feeling. He had almost *composed*; and his composition had embraced the truth." This composition of life by means of knowledge, imagination, and feeling is the artist's task. He works from his observations to give us a vision of reality more structured, more vividly crystallized, than we can make in our lives, and hence one capable of being deeper and truer. The reason James uses the style and tone he does in this story, the reason he will go on to explore in stylistic techniques, is that he is trying to make the reader see for himself. He does not tell us what reality is, but he shows us the many visions of it; and by consciously composing, imaginatively playing scenes one against another, by using stylistic techniques to move us beneath appearances, he creates a medium through which we can evaluate the various levels of reality and make a judgment. Such an interpretation of reality as a many-sided phenomenon is a complex

process that leads, quite naturally, to the endlessly inconclusive questioning that becomes the central concern of
the late novel, *The Sacred Fount*. What, finally, is real,
and who is to say? The answers, even in this novel, seem
to be the artist and his vision, or at least the work of art
into which he shapes that vision. But as the novel suggests, the finer the artist's vision of life becomes, the
more various is what he sees; he too is caught with the
problem of defining reality in its complexity—he too is
human.

James creates what seems an equivocal scene—an example of the problem of defining reality—when he presents Baxter's fiancée looking at the finished portrait of
Marian. The fiancée is a "black-haired girl of twenty,
with irregular features, a pair of luminous dark eyes, and
a smile radiant of white teeth—evidently an excellent
person. She turned to Lennox with a look of frank sympathy, and said in a deep, rich voice . . ." (I, 293). It is
she who makes a distinction between art and life: " 'I
know Mr. Baxter is a genius. But what is a picture, at the
best? I've seen nothing but pictures for the last two
years, and I haven't seen a single pretty girl' " (I, 293).
For a moment after this remark her face, so clearly
radiating for Lennox the depth that Marian lacks,
merges for him with the face on the canvas and suggests
an ideal to Lennox. Of course, Lennox does not realize
he might again be duped by a female, one James says has
"a smile radiant of white teeth—evidently an excellent
person"—a remark that may be highly facetious. On the
other hand, James might be suggesting that the appearance of Baxter's fiancée to Lennox is actually an ideal—
art refines on life, as does the portrait, and then life
refines on art, as does the fiancée standing in front of the
portrait. James is still a young, immature writer, and he
is not certain of art, nor has he yet committed himself to
a life of art. Perhaps this scene is his way of hedging his

uncertainty. In any event, Baxter's fiancée and her re-mark seem suggestive and equivocal, and the reader is left uncertain as to what is real. Perhaps—to suggest another level of reality—it is these many possible levels of interpretation of reality that James means to suggest by this peculiar scene.

In the end Lennox marries Marian, knowing what she is and what can be expected from her. His willingness to do so indicates his implicit acceptance of the surface values his society recognizes and he questions but cannot give up. Because this vision of life is too much for Lennox, he marries and destroys the masterpiece that gave him this vision. Art can make us see, but we cannot always accept what we see. What ultimately happens to Lennox, James leaves unstated. He has given us an impression of the complex, sometimes frightening, mystery of life; but he cannot, as William James said in his letter, conclude or "finish" this mystery. It goes on.

As an American artist himself, James can only create careful portraits of his society that will be interpreted variously, depending on one's point of view, on how much one "sees." There is nothing cruel in James's intention, but there is something critical, sharp, precise, and, most importantly, real. What one sees in this tale is, finally, *in* the amount one sees in life, in one's point of view. John Lennox has failed because of his failure to move out of his social forms and observe what appears before him, and then to risk his life for an experience broader than these forms. Marian Everett is an embodiment of the beautiful vacuity of that society. Only the artist, removed, observing, just returned from Europe, is capable of seeing and shaping meaning, and then only in his art. He states his moral in his portrait of the light woman. Such a vision, such an art, is too much for this world and must be destroyed.

Although the vision of this tale is the vision of a work

of art expressing and shaping life, perhaps this vision, as it must be destroyed, is also too much for the young, uncertain James. He needs more confidence in his own ability to see and in his art before he commits himself. He goes to Europe, and there, after returning twice to America, he accepts the life of the artist. In doing so he clarifies his relation to art, a relation that is not altogether certain in "The Story of a Masterpiece." He accepts the artist's vision as the one he will pursue and elevate in society as valid, significant, and essential, for it is the artist's vision that is generous and sophisticated, truly international.

2

The Apprentice Years—Morality in Europe: 1868–1872

James's first adult journey to Europe lasted only from February, 1869, to May, 1870, but the imprint of this experience was indelible. He returned to Cambridge, Massachusetts, and for two years longed for the quality of life he had found in Europe.[1] A comment from his Preface to *The Reverberator* explains what James thought his attitude to be at this time.

> A part of that adventure [of traveling abroad] had been the never-to-be-forgotten thrill of a first sight of Italy, from late in the summer of 1869 on; so that a return to America at the beginning of the following year was to drag with it, as a lengthening chain, the torment of losses and regrets. The repatriated victim of that unrest was, beyond doubt, acutely conscious of his case: the fifteen months just spent in Europe had absolutely determined his situation. The nostalgic poison had been distilled for him, the future presented to him but as a single intense question: was he to spend it in brooding exile, or might he somehow come into his "own"?—as I liked betimes to put it for a romantic analogy with the state of dispossessed princes and wandering heirs. The question was to answer itself promptly enough—yet after a delay sufficient to give me the measure of a whole previous relation to it.[2]

During this "delay sufficient," and shortly before, James wrote several of his early and experimental tales.

"Osborne's Revenge" (1868), "A Light Man" (1869), and "Gabrielle de Bergerac" (1869) were written before James left on his trip. They are his preparatory steps away from the limitations he saw in America toward the life he imagined in Europe. The first two are social criticism of the quality of American life; the last is a European-centered story, a historical tale of life just before the French Revolution. The titles of the tales set in Europe and written after his return from there in 1870 reveal James's preoccupation with being abroad: "Travelling Companions" (1870), "A Passionate Pilgrim" (1871), and "At Isella" (1871). Two further tales written during this period are set in America: "Master Eustace" (1871) and "Guest's Confession" (1872). At the time these last tales were written James attempted his first novel, *Watch and Ward*, which was serialized in the *Atlantic* from August to December, 1871. This novel, which James did not publish as a book until 1878 and did not want recognized, is set in America but reflects in part James's European predilection during this period: the heroine is sent to Rome to be educated, and the novel contains lengthy and evocative correspondence from her about the experience.[3]

James's work during this period is ambivalent, at times poorly written, and often naïve and uncritical. Although some of the tales of this period might be biographically important and even appeal to James—he republished "A Passionate Pilgrim" as the title story in his first published collection of tales; it is the earliest tale included in the New York Edition—none of the tales of this period is successful. Two, "A Light Man" and "Gabrielle de Bergerac," present potentially interesting narratives unsuccessfully handled, but most suffer from uninteresting situations that are poorly written. James is shifting his center of interest from America to Europe, and his writing reflects an uncertain movement toward his international theme. However, in their experimental simplicity and in their groping toward his international theme, these youthful tales blatantly reveal the early and tentative development of James's important concept of morality.

This concept of morality is unusual. The basis of it is found in four quotations, diverse in origin but related to this early period of James's life. The first is from James's autobiography, *A Small Boy and Others*. He is discussing his father and his family. It is followed by a passage James wrote in 1863 when he was twenty, and by two quotations by Henry James Senior: one from a letter and one from the brief autobiography written by the novelist's father.

> I can scarce sufficiently express how little it [our family] could have conduced to the formation of prigs. Our father's prime horror was of *them*—he only cared for virtue that was more or less ashamed of itself; and nothing could have been of a happier whimsicality than the mixture in him . . . of the strongest instinct for the human and the liveliest reaction from the literal. The literal played in our education as small a part as it perhaps ever played in any, and we wholesomely breathed inconsistency and ate and drank contradictions. . . . The moral of all of which was that we need never fear not to be good enough if we were only social enough: a splendid meaning indeed being attached to the latter term.

> Thus we had ever the amusement, since I can really call it nothing less, of hearing morality, or moralism, as it was more invidiously worded, made hay of in the very interest of character and conduct; these things suffering much, it seemed, by their association with the conscience—that is the *conscious* conscience—the very home of the literal, the haunt of so many pedantries.[4]
>
> A SMALL BOY AND OTHERS

We were certainly born to believe. The truth was certainly made to be believed. Life is a prolonged reconciliation of these two facts. As long as we squint at the truth instead of looking straight at it—*i.e.* as long as we are prejudiced instead of fair, so long are we miserable sinners. But it seems to me that this fatal obliquity of vision inheres not wholly in any individual but is some indefinable property in the social atmosphere. —When by some concerted movement of humanity the air is purified then the film will fall from our eyes and (to conclude gracefully) we shall gaze undazzled at the sun!!!! [5]

LETTER TO THOMAS SERGEANT PERRY

I hate tyranny, and spiritual tyranny above all other forms of it, i.e. the tyranny that prevails against you by availing itself of your ignorance or prejudice in respect to truth, and so putting you in hopeless conflict with yourself.

HENRY JAMES SENIOR

They [the worldly mind and the religious mind] thus conflict with the principles of universal justice . . . which rigidly enjoins that *each particular thing exist for all, and that all things in general exist for each.* Our family at all events perfectly illustrated this common vice of contented isolation. Like all the other families of the land it gave no sign of a *spontaneous* religious culture, or of affections touched to the dimensions of universal man.[6]

HENRY JAMES SENIOR

The last quotation appears in Henry James Senior's discussion of his own early family life. He objected to the upbringing his father gave him, which was Calvinistic, self-centered, and restrictive. Henry Senior believed all organized forms of Christianity destroyed man's freedom and spontaneity. He became an independent Christian and an extreme social democrat, one who seriously advocated socialism as the proper condition for man.[7] He instilled in his children a high degree of individuality and a liberal social consciousness, one, however, that had little relationship to existing institutions and conventions. As a result there was a conflict between the highly individualistic nature of the James children and their socialistic consciousness, as well as between their unconventional beliefs and the more conventional ones of the majority of society—both conflicts in part accounting for the genius and perhaps even neurotic frustrations of the James children. They were themselves the specially aware human beings that Henry James writes about.

The relationship between the first remark by Henry Junior and the last by Henry Senior might be apparent. "The moral of all of which was that we need never fear not to be good enough if we were only social enough: a splendid meaning indeed being attached to the latter term"; and that splendid meaning: *each particular thing exist for all, and that all things in general exist for each.*" Henry James's liberal social education is the opposite of his father's narrow and restrictive experience. The education of Henry Junior produces a morality that is social ("each particular thing . . . for all . . . all things in general exist for each"), that insists on "the dimensions of universal man," not on the particular man. This universality is found when man does not succumb to the spiritual tyranny of "ignorance or prejudice in respect to truth," but looks "straight at" the truth in his life. Then comes the recognition that all men share in life only to the degree that they fully sense their social relationship and interdependence. In that realization one can begin to understand life, to become what James most admired: finely aware and richly responsible.

> This in fact I have ever found rather terribly the point —that the figures in any picture, the agents in any drama, are interesting only in proportion as they feel their respective situations; since the consciousness, on their part, of the complication exhibited forms for us their link of

connexion with it. But there are degrees of feeling—the muffled, the faint, the just sufficient, the barely intelligent, as we may say; and the acute, the intense, the complete, in a word—the power to be finely aware and richly responsible. It is those moved in this latter fashion who "get most" out of all that happens to them and who in so doing enable us, as readers of their record, as participators by a fond attention, also to get most. Their being finely aware—as Hamlet and Lear, say, are finely aware—*makes* absolutely the intensity of their adventure, gives the maximum of sense to what befalls them.[8]

Morality for Henry James is not priggishness—to feel one's superiority in doing the right thing—but to see and feel one's actions as part of a social sphere. Character and conduct are not measured by restrictive and definitive codes of right and wrong, but by the amount of feeling the individual possesses—his grasp on the reality. In one of the eight tales under discussion in this chapter, "Travelling Companions," James says: " 'We ought to learn from all this to be *real* . . . to discriminate between genuine and factitious sentiment; between the substantial and the trivial; between the essential and the superfluous; sentiment and sentimentality' " (II, 210–11). If man sees and feels fully the social reality, he will act sensitively.[9] Morality is truly social. The moral life, the one well lived, is that in which man deeply feels and is most fully aware of social relationships and least emphasizes the particularity of difference that separates him and limits his vision. The concept is democratic and pragmatic, which certainly relates Henry to William James.[10]

The repercussion of these ideas in James's writing is significant. If James in his fiction is mostly concerned with the manners and style of the more sensitive and intelligent individuals of society, it is because they should be more potentially capable of being finely aware of the social experience. He concentrates on those freed of social restraints, such as the absence of money, in part because they should be freer to be aware of the universal element that unites man rather than the mundane particulars that separate him. James is concerned less and less with the ordinary incidents of life, with narrative events as we normally conceive of them, and more with the amount of felt and universally relevant life to be found behind these. The particulars of the narratives are means and, as such, essential to lead us to what is "behind," but they are only means. It makes little difference *what* you examine as a writer, but it does matter what your examination *leads* you to. If, for instance, the artistic experience and the supernatural are by nature concerned with the realm of the universal—of truth, of the nonmaterial—then the particulars *of* art and the supernatural are excellent means to lead to this universal. Style becomes increasingly important, since it is a means to express one's awareness of what does lie behind the surface and is a means to the reader's movement into the sphere beyond the particular. Events and language become more abstract as one moves closer to the universal statement. This same idea is put another way by James in 1885: "*Life* seems to mean moral and intellectual and spiritual life, and not the everlasting vulgar chapters of accidents, the dead rattle and rumble, which rise from the mere surface of things." [11]

Given this definition, morality in art is like morality in life: each is a question for James of the felt life involved. A quotation from the Preface to *The Portrait of a Lady* can be related to the above quotations and should help to make this relationship clear, a relationship that grew as James developed as a writer:

There is, I think, no more nutritive or suggestive truth . . . than that of the perfect dependence of the "moral" sense of a work of art on the amount of felt life concerned in producing it. The question comes back thus, obviously, to the kind and the degree of the artist's prime sensibility, which is the soil out of which his subject springs. The quality and capacity of that soil, its ability to "grow" with due freshness and straightness any vision of life, represents, strongly or weakly, the projected morality. That element is but another name for the more or less close connexion of the subject with some mark made on the intelligence, with some sincere experience.[12]

It is possible to return now to the group of tales James wrote between 1868 and 1872 to see how they reveal the hesitant and early development of this morality in James's fiction. The eight tales are examinations of the inability of people to see beyond those particulars of their lives that distort their vision. A man sees what his friend wants him to see, which is not true, and finally discovers his friend was mad ("Osborne's Revenge"). A man trusts his friend until he learns that this friend, while in Europe, has adopted a cynical materialism that allows him to deceive ruthlessly ("A Light Man"). Two young people must assert their love against a corrupt society that interprets this love as grossly immoral ("Gabrielle de Bergerac"). The appearance of two American lovers in Europe is thought to be immoral, and they cannot marry until they accept their own truth and ignore what European society thinks ("Travelling Companions"). An American's view of America and Europe is distorted by his painfully unbalanced mind ("A Passionate Pilgrim"). An American boy is so spoiled by his mother that he refuses to accept reality and truth ("Master Eustace"). A silly young man must learn to grow up and away from his family and to accept a more complex vision of life ("Guest's Confession").[13]

The narrative situations of these tales are those of a young man. They are all concerned with growing up, friendship, first love, finding what one believes in. What is interesting about these tales is the relationships James examines: friends deceive friends; young people love despite the restrictions of society; Europe represents a society radically different from America; immaturity and failure to leave the family distort one's sense of the truth. James is looking at certain of the conventions of life we most often consider fundamental. There are eight stories: two on deception in friendship, two on deception in love caused by the restrictions of society, two on deception caused by the limitations of convention and environment, two on deception caused by immaturity and a refusal to break the family bond. In each tale, once the individual removes himself from his limited position, he immediately comes to a new understanding of his relationship with other people that transcends his limited vision and makes him aware of a reality and truth that he had not seen before. In this process his life becomes broader, deeper, and richer; he becomes moral to the degree that he feels life.

That James sees in Europe a morality different from that in America is evident from "A Light Man," "Gabrielle de Bergerac," and the other tales set in Europe, particularly "A Passionate Pilgrim," which is based on the awareness of the distinct moral difference between America and Europe. But James does not yet fully understand this contrast that will eventually so effectively express his moral vision. He could not, really, be expected to without the experimentation of writing these tales that helps him to examine the characteristics in the contrast. That Europe is used in eleven of the nineteen tales James had written by 1872 shows James's strong European orientation. Europe is the setting of five of these eleven tales. In the other six it is of an importance varying from the insignificant departure of Gertrude Whittaker to Florence at the end of "Poor Richard" (1867), to the European atmosphere of the American household in "De Grey: A Romance" (1868), to the significant influence of Europe upon the character of Maximus Austin in "A Light Man" (1869). This last tale—one written during the period examined here—is really the first "international" tale James wrote, and a study of it will help us to understand what the European contrast means to James as he begins to form it and how the Jamesian meaning of morality is fundamental to it.

Maximus Austin returns from Europe as a seeker of pleasure, a professed pagan who measures everything according to his own desires. He finds his friend's Christian simplicity oppressive. This friend, Theodore, lacks all modulation, color, and tone; he is so naïve as not even to be aware of his own behavior or of Max's obvious deceptions. Each sees the world in his own peculiar way and sees nothing more. The two pay court to an old and rich man, an erratic fool of vain caprices who has spent most of his life in Europe, although he is an American. In the end neither Theodore nor Max obtains the old man's fortune, but there is a good chance Max will marry the niece who has inherited the money.

Already in this story is the contrast between America and Europe that James is later to develop so superbly. It is too simply and blatantly put, but the story is sustained by this contrast as it is embodied in the two young men. Neither of them emerges as admirable. They both lack any degree of moral depth, since they are too tied to their particular visions. The old man is almost a caricature of the old fool. He has missed too much of life in his shallow existence, and now, King Lear-like, he plays the wanton boy and tries to make up for his past. He is a mixture of both young men, of America and Europe. One can see in him the naïve Christian and the pagan materialist, the man of no shadows and the man of molded surfaces and dark crevices, the man of naïveté and the deceiver. The question the tale asks is, who is the light man? It appears at first that it is the pagan Maximus since James uses Max's diary to reveal his crassness, but Theodore is really no better. He is just as eager for the inheritance, only not as aware of his means of obtaining it. And the old man is so inconsequential that he can do nothing but parody what each of them is thinking and doing. All three, because of their restrictive and shallow vision, are light, weak men.

"A Light Man" is not a successful tale. It introduces too many subjects that are not adequately discussed: materialism, ambition, America-Europe, Christianity-paganism. It also suffers from several passages that have unintentional sexual overtones, none as pathetically obvious as those in *Watch and Ward*,[14] but still disturbingly naïve.[15] Although the tale establishes different relationships, they are as odd as those in *Watch and Ward*.[16] "A Light Man" was written shortly before *Watch and Ward*, and one feels that James is using his fiction to examine, unconsciously, certain sexual questions. In the future sex is a matter James largely excludes from fiction as not a fit subject, one to be left to the privacy of individuals. If he includes it, he presents it almost abstractly, centering not on its particulars, but on how a sexual encounter, such as that between the Prince and Charlotte Stant in *The Golden Bowl*, affects the lives of those involved.

The tale does show, in Max, an early version of the materialistic European-American who is epitomized in Gilbert Osmond; Theodore seems a very early and undeveloped Lambert Strether; and the old man is a mixture of Abel Gaw and Frank Betterman, the two old, rich men in *The Ivory Tower*. Essentially, however, the tale is important in its use of the international contrast to express the Jamesian morality: the particular, limited viewpoint, either American or European, is not enough; the moral man, the man who is not "light," is the one freed of narrow restraints, the one who combines the best, whether of America or Europe.

Probably it is this contrasting moral viewpoint on America and Europe, even though inadequately stated, that made "A Passionate Pilgrim" appeal to James. James says as much, admitting the tale's weakness and personal claim, in his Preface to the tale in the New York Edition.

> "A Passionate Pilgrim," written in the year 1870, the earliest date to which anything in the whole present series refers itself, strikes me to-day, and by the same token indescribably touches me, with the two compositions that follow it, as sops instinctively thrown to the international Cerberus formidably posted where I doubtless then didn't quite make him out, yet from whose capacity to loom larger and larger with the years there must already have sprung some chilling portent.
>
> As I read over "A Passionate Pilgrim" and "The Madonna of the Future" they become in the highest degree documentary for myself—from all measure of such interest as they may possibly have at this time of day for others I stand off; though I disengage from them but one thing, their betrayal of their consolatory use. The deep beguilement of the lost vision recovered, in comparative indigence, by a certain inexpert intensity of art—the service rendered by them at need, with whatever awkwardness and difficulty—sticks out of them for me to the exclusion of everything else and consecrates them, I freely admit, to memory.[17]

This statement seems to be a valid analysis of the tale. It has primarily a personal claim and significance. It is true that in this tale James begins to sharpen his international perspective in the contrast between the failure of American society to provide color and subtlety and the failure of European society to provide opportunity and freedom. The hero, Clement Searle, is the deprived

American seeking the richness of Europe. Miss Searle, his distant English relative, and a destitute Englishman represent aspirations for freedom and America. Richard Searle, another English relative, represents the failure of European culture to exhibit the quality expected of it. What is annoying about the tale is James's ambivalent attitude, so representative of his own condition at this time. He cannot decide whether we are to admire or despise Clement Searle. This must in part be the "inexpert intensity of art" he speaks of. Searle is portrayed as a pathetic and romantic madman, yet he represents an attitude James insists has some validity. What is wrong is not James's desire to see values in both America and Europe—his impartiality is an important element in his international theme—but his failure here to know what he wants to say and to find fictional means to express successfully his theme. Clement Searle must be mad to be possible—and even as a madman his actions are sometimes unintentionally humorous instead of pathetic—but as mad he cannot be taken as representative. If he is driven mad by American society, the weakness is in his limited intellectual sensitivity as much as in American society. It is difficult not to find this tale, for all its exciting description and personal conviction, the ineffectual work of a young writer struggling to express his theme. It shows James's failure to clearly delineate the elements in this theme because of his too particular, noninternational vision.[18]

One can find in William James partial explanation for Henry's inclination toward Europe. William wrote to his brother Robertson about Henry on January 2, 1870, while Henry was still on his first adult journey in Europe: "I fear his taste of Europe will prevent his ever getting thoroughly reconciled to his country and I imagine that he will end, when he becomes self-supporting, by spending most of his time there. Certainly with his artistic temperament and literary occupations, I should not blame him for the choice." [19]

The direction was not just a matter of personal comfort and taste. James can also be seen as deliberately removing himself from the particularity that appears in "A Passionate Pilgrim," in order to eliminate the immature weaknesses as a writer that are found in "A Light Man," and to put himself into the truly moral, artistic life as he saw it, one that would eventually make possible the fine international tales he would write. "A Passionate Pilgrim" is a personal story for James, as his own comments indicate, and a statement from that tale can be seen as advice to himself to begin to lead this moral life. The narrator of "A Passionate Pilgrim" says to the American, Clement Searle: " 'You have lived hitherto in yourself. The tenement's haunted! Live abroad! Take an interest' " (II, 247). James himself does this. He is free to do so because he is an American. It is in a letter to Thomas Sergeant Perry that James makes this point.

We are Americans born—*il faut en prendre son parti*. I look upon it as a great blessing; and I think that to be an American is an excellent preparation for culture. We have exquisite qualities as a race, and it seems to me that we are ahead of the European races in the fact that more than either of them we can deal freely with forms of civilization not our own, can pick and choose and assimilate and in short (aesthetically &c) claim our property wherever we find it. To have no national stamp has hitherto been a regret & a drawback, but I think it not unlikely that American writers may yet indicate that a vast intellectual fusion and synthesis of the various National tendencies of the world is the condition of more important achievements than any we have seen. We must of course have something of our own—something distinctive & homogeneous—& I take it that we shall find it in our moral consciousness, our unprecedented spiritual lightness and vigour. In this sense at least we shall have a national *cachet.*—I expect nothing great during your lifetime or mine perhaps; but my instincts quite agree with yours in looking to see something original and beautiful disengage itself from our ceaseless fermentation and turmoil. You see I am willing to leave it a matter of instinct.[20]

James believes Americans are free to fuse and synthesize, as no other people can—when they are willing to do so. They are the most potentially moral people in the world. He uses this potential freedom as an American *and* his career as a writer to find the moral life: both allow him to live as he wants, emotionally and creatively. The result is an American writer who chooses to live in Europe. Although Europe has its own particularities, it provides one decisive and early step away from the particularity of America—out of a tenement that is haunted for James. Another letter to Perry, one already mentioned, points out the moral commitment in James's decision to live abroad: "As long as we squint at the truth instead of looking straight at it—*i.e.* as long as we are prejudiced instead of fair, so long we are miserable sinners. But it seems to me that this fatal obliquity of vision inheres not wholly in any individual but is some indefinable property in the social atmosphere. —When by some concerted movement of humanity the air is purified then the film will fall from our eyes and ('conclude gracefully) we shall gaze undazzled at the sun!!!!" [21]

Once we understand the moral vision that James is seeking—one that transcends the particulars of individuals, societies, and nations—we are able to understand why he so often insists in his international tales, or in his tales of artists and his ghost stories, not on one view, but on a multiple vision, removed from the literal—one closer to the realm of morality as he interprets it. To express such a vision in art becomes his purpose.[22]

One of the tales of this period particularly illustrates

the unusual and disparate forces that are a part of this vision of James. "Gabrielle de Bergerac" is set in eighteenth-century France and is concerned with the American Revolution, the decay of the French aristocracy, and the coming French uprising. Pierre Coquelin, poor and lowly born, but well educated, the tutor to a nobleman's son, has fought in the American Revolution. Only he can speak of what it means, as only he can "speak" to the peasants and the noblemen. James gives him the articulate voice and breadth of vision he associates with the artist; and, in fact, Pierre is a painter. It is the existence of a brilliant portrait of his wife that prompts the telling of the tale, many years after the events. Pierre, in his position as tutor, meets the nobleman's sister, Gabrielle de Bergerac. They, with the truth of their love, break through the lifeless forms of their decaying world and marry. Pierre and Gabrielle are a microcosm of the fine, new world that judges not by what must be but by what is. They die in the French Revolution because their voice, James suggests, is too subtle a combination to be heard; as artists of life, as true moralists, they are not understood. The aristocracy consider them immoral and the people are suspicious of them.

One can see James dealing with several themes. There is the end of an old social condition and its attitudes and the creation of a new society with a new vision. James clearly admires the democratic revolutions that allow man to be seen for what he is. At the same time James acknowledges the excess of these events; they are hopelessly destructive of the good they create. It is in the delicate, free blending of the life, intellect, and vision of a Pierre Coquelin with the sensitivity, breeding, and courage of a Gabrielle de Bergerac that the moral condition comes into being. James puts the story in the past, away from him, as if he could not see the condition in his own environment, but he is, nonetheless, certain of what he means. Against Pierre is set a French aristocrat who wants to marry Gabrielle, but he is, for all his fineness, too effete a specimen; he is decadent, foppish, elegant to excess, and not intelligent. Pierre is everything he is not. When Pierre is asked by Gabrielle about his philosophy, he replies, almost as Lambert Strether will some thirty years later, " 'It's a very old one. It's simply to make the most of life while it lasts. I'm very fond of life' " (II, 140).

The moral attitude of this tale is not in its surface examination of an aristocratic society, but it is in the fine symbolic quality of the characters and the situation. Man must take life into his hands, structure his reality like a work of art, freely, finely, and without fear. He must not be parochial, in any sense. "Gabrielle de Bergerac" is concerned with the "international" vision that comes to the man who looks out at his world with truth, passion, intelligence, and courage. This is the vision of an aristocratic democrat. Such a man is an artist of life, a moral man, and it is his condition, the quality of his consciousness, that James now begins to assume himself and to consider as the central theme of his work.

3

The International Style: 1873–1875

During the summer of 1873 when Henry James was thirty, he wrote "Madame de Mauves," a tale of an American woman married to a French baron. The story is told from the point of view of an American who falls in love with her, and although it is called after the woman, the tale is as well an account of the American's slowly developing awareness of himself and those around him.

A character through whose consciousness the events are sifted is a structural device James uses in his second novel, *Roderick Hudson*, which he wrote shortly after "Madame de Mauves" and first published in 1875. As he acknowledges in his 1907 Preface to this novel, James considers Rowland Mallet to be the subject of *Roderick Hudson*.

> My subject, all blissfully, in face of difficulties, had defined itself—and this in spite of the title of the book—as not directly, in the least, my young sculptor's adventure. This it had been but indirectly, being all the while in essence and in final effect another man's, his friend's and patron's, view and experience of him.[1]

This is not the only similarity between the tale and the novel. Both show James beginning to handle with assurance his important international theme and its contrasting faces: America and Europe, good and evil, vulgarity and refinement, freedom and restriction, renunciation and fulfillment. As the theme is refined by James in these works, he uses it to show the contrast between art and life, discipline and spontaneity. It finally resolves into a structural element that can express the ambivalent qualities of any nature. When James found this dramatic and expressive structure in the very elements of his international theme, he also found greater stylistic control and symbolic power.

"Madame de Mauves" is the earliest extended example of the development of this complex structure.[2] In this tale Longmore, an American visiting in Europe, meets Madame de Mauves through an American acquaintance, Mrs. Draper. Euphemia de Mauves, who is married to a Frenchman of an old and distinguished family, fascinates Longmore with her beauty and reserve. They become friends, but Longmore, in apparent deference to her strong and dominant character and her peculiar sadness, does not pursue her ardently, only properly. It is revealed that the Baron de Mauves has married Euphemia for her money and now has a mistress. First his widowed sister, Madame Clairin, attempts to attach herself to Longmore, for his money, and later to suggest —at her brother's instigation—that Longmore have an affair with Madame de Mauves. Such an affair, it is indicated, would relieve the Baron of any guilt. The affair does not take place, although Longmore *seems* to desire it. At Madame de Mauves' request Longmore leaves for America, making clear to the Baron and his sister that Madame de Mauves and he are not intimately involved. Longmore goes only because her request is so grandly irrefutable. Madame de Mauves' apparent devotion to her husband causes the Baron to love her again, and he repents his folly. Longmore hears, through Mrs. Draper, who has it indirectly from Madame Clairin, that the Baron, in desperation at his wife's refusal to accept his repentance, has blown out his brains. When Longmore hears the news, he does not return to France to see Madame de Mauves: "The truth is, that in the midst of all the ardent tenderness of his memory of Madame de Mauves, he has become conscious of a singular feeling, —a feeling for which awe would be hardly too strong a name" (III, 209).

When first read, the tale might appear to be the account of a puritanical American woman married to a decadent Frenchman, seen through the eyes of an admiring and distant American. Any moral questions can be dealt with fairly simply and cleanly: The Baron de Mauves' suicide is what one might expect of him and no more than he deserves for his blatant adultery; Madame de Mauves is hard, but acts as she justifiably might in the situation. Of course there is much more to the tale, and we are at once given a suggestion of this in the name of the principal character. Madame de Mauves is born Euphemia *Cleve*. She attends a convent school, and James shows that she is a victim of the same romantic illusions and sentiments that affect Emma Bovary during and after her convent education. It would seem that James is deliberately suggesting certain parallels to two of the most famous women in French fiction—Madame de La Fayette's Princesse de Clèves and Flaubert's Madame Bovary—and by doing so expanding the tale's scope and significance.

Apart from her maiden name, Cleve, Madame de Mauves has certain other attributes in common with Madame de La Fayette's Princesse de Clèves. Euphemia de Mauves' husband has his country place in Auvergne, the same part of France in which Madame de La Fayette's husband lived and from which she fled to live in Paris. In James's tale the situation is reversed and Madame de Mauves flees to Auvergne. The choice of the names "Cleve" and "Auvergne" seems too much for coincidence, but there is a similarity that is greater: both the Princesse de Clèves and Madame de Mauves act from the principle of duty and in the process kill their husbands, deny their lovers, and end senselessly hidden from the life they desire, one in a convent and the other deep in the country. Both works are subtly conceived moralistic attacks upon corrupt society, but both condemn the virtuous woman as much as the corrupt society. Or at least the Princesse de Clèves is so condemned, and one can also condemn Euphemia. We are led to believe it is Madame de Mauves' refusal to accept her repentant husband that causes his death. Certainly, no matter how immoral he was, her refusal to accept his repentance shows a hardness of spirit that demands examination. One can only pity a woman whose concept of life is so fantastic—so romantically perfect—as to deny reality and kill life.[3]

It is this last point that relates Madame de Mauves to Madame Bovary. Each woman is moved by her convent education and romantic nature to conceive in life an ideal that only exists in her mind. They choose different ways to live, but in the end they have become pathetic and destructive women, far from what they ideally and impossibly desire. Both are victims not only of themselves but of the society that forms them. Madame de Mauves is for James the puritan American limited by her restrictive principles, and Madame Bovary is destroyed by the mediocrity of the French provincial society she cannot transcend.

We can be certain of James's interest in Flaubert's masterpiece, since he expressed great admiration for it—and for its moral value—in an essay published in 1876.[4] Flaubert's remark, "Madame Bovary, c'est moi," could also be said by James about Madame de Mauves. Her perfect control and aura, her irrefutable perseverance of an ideal, are qualities one can imagine James admiring *and* disliking in himself. He is fascinated by her purity and idealism as an American woman, but knows that they fix limitations on life that are unreal and restrictive.

The inclination to avoid in reading this tale is to center attention only on Madame de Mauves. This approach, understandable considering the title, is not so wrong as it is limiting, since it tends to exclude consideration of the character of Longmore.[5] One might think of him only as the consciousness used to relate Euphemia's story and of no inherent importance. If an awareness of James's later and significant use of this structural consciousness in *Roderick Hudson, The Portrait of a Lady,* and *The Ambassadors* does not suggest his possible further intention in "Madame de Mauves," then Longmore's importance in the tale should be made clear by the scene in which he takes a long walk in the country, falls asleep, and dreams. This sequence in which only Longmore figures prominently is the most carefully articulated statement of the tale's complex meaning.

Longmore goes to the country to ponder the troubled state of his relationship with Euphemia. There seems no solution; he is frustrated in love. In the green and lush setting, he finds an artist living with a beautiful woman. They seem extremely happy in their idyllic world. He is told by an innkeeper that they are not married, and she leads him to believe that the relationship might not last. Longmore comes to realize that the lovers' eventual separation is not significant, since the two are in love now, but Longmore senses his own emotional inadequacy in the face of such naturalness. At the end of the sequence he falls asleep and dreams that he cannot cross a river to Euphemia who is on the other side. He is afraid to plunge into the water, and when a mysterious man takes him across, Euphemia is then on the opposite side. The mysterious man, he discovers, is the Baron de Mauves.

This incident in the country and the dream are particularly interesting in that they show James's awareness of an area he is usually thought to evade: sex and sexual fantasy. The sequence is a brilliant combination of the reality and fantasy of sexual encounter. It is important to understand that the sexual quality in the scene is *not* incidental to the meaning of the tale.

Longmore is portrayed as weak and ineffectual. He is the inexperienced American male who has not had contact with the realities of life and is at first naïvely shocked to find the artist and his woman unmarried, although that realization does not bring forth a moral condemnation, only moral confusion. Before this scene the reader might have wondered why Longmore has been so evasive in speaking of his love to Madame de Mauves. He would, at first, not admit his deep passion, and then he would not act upon it. In America, we are led to believe, he had not experienced the passion that would show him how to act. As a man he is indecisive and ineffectual.

In the dream one sees the symbolic implications of Longmore's character. He will not *plunge* into the *deep water* to reach Euphemia. He fears he will *lose* sight of her, perhaps *drown* himself. He is taken across the water, but by then she is on the *other* side, on the side he was originally on. The man who takes him is the husband who has finally suggested he have an affair. The implication seems to be that if Longmore had acted on his own soon enough, he might have had a relationship with Euphemia similar to the one between the artist and his woman. He does not have it because he is not aware of what he is doing until too late. The dream is a representation of the reality, potential and then actual; in it one sees the full implications of Longmore's weakness.

It could be assumed that what James most admires in this sequence is Longmore's romantic vision of the idyllic and simple country, as if it, and not the relationship that takes place in it, were an image of the ideal life. To assume that the love affair is not James's ideal is to ignore much in this scene. It appears more likely that the relationship between the artist and his woman is the natural representation in life of the vibrancy shown in nature. The fact that we see the story through Longmore's consciousness does not mean that we take his remarks as fact and do not judge him as well, in the contrast between what he sees and thinks and what we see and think. We are certainly not meant to be as childishly surprised by the couple as Longmore. Also, in ignoring the importance of the lovers in this scene, one tends to ignore the sexual implications in the dream, implying that the sequence has not been seriously conceived by James. What James implies in this section, and throughout the tale, is that Longmore's consciousness never becomes truly aware; it only approaches awareness. Even at the end of the tale, Longmore is only in "awe" of Madame de Mauves. Longmore never sees her nor himself because he is the ineffectual and insensitive male whom James exposes in actuality by his inaction and figuratively by his dream.

Perhaps we can better understand this scene by looking at certain specific passages. The scene occupies all of Section VII of the tale—there are nine sections in all— and takes place right after Longmore has been informed by Madame Clairin, the Baron's sister, that he might have an affair with Madame de Mauves. Here is James's description of Longmore as he moves toward the country:

> He felt immensely excited, but he could hardly have said whether his emotion was a pain or a joy. It was joyous as all increase of freedom is joyous; something seemed to have been knocked down across his path; his destiny appeared to have rounded a cape and brought him into

sight of an open sea. But his freedom resolved itself
somehow into the need of despising all mankind, with a
single exception; and the fact of Madame de Mauves
inhabiting a planet contaminated by the presence of this
baser multitude kept his elation from seeming a pledge of
ideal bliss.

But she was there, and circumstance now forced them
to be intimate. She had ceased to have what men call a
secret for him, and this fact itself brought with it a sort of
rapture. He had no prevision that he should "profit," in
the vulgar sense, by the extraordinary position into which
they had been thrown; it might be but a cruel trick of
destiny to make hope a harsher mockery and renunciation
a keener suffering. But above all this rose the conviction
that she could do nothing that would not deepen his
admiration.

It was this feeling that circumstance—unlovely as it was
in itself—was to force the beauty of her character into
more perfect relief, that made him stride along as if he
were celebrating a kind of spiritual festival. He rambled at
random for a couple of hours, and found at last that he
had left the forest behind him and had wandered into an
unfamiliar region. It was a perfectly rural scene, and the
still summer day gave it a charm for which its meagre
elements but half accounted. (III, 182–83)

The full ambiguity of the scene is in this description,
but were it not for what we have seen of Longmore,
what he further sees in this scene, and the dream, we
might assume that James is deliberately setting up a
nonsexual, romantic ideal. One can see in this description what is thought of as the typical, too refined, and
emasculated Jamesian situation—although an indication
of what is to come is clearly given here: "he had left the
forest behind him and had wandered into an unfamiliar
region." Immediately after this passage James makes it
clear that he is showing Longmore in an unusual and
significant situation that is highly provocative.

The homely tavern sounds coming out through the open windows, the sunny stillness of the fields and crops, which covered so much vigorous natural life, suggested very little that was transcendental, had very little to say about re-nunciation,—nothing at all about spiritual zeal. They seemed to utter a message from plain ripe nature, to express the unperverted reality of things, to say that the common lot is not brilliantly amusing, and that the part of wisdom is to grasp frankly at experience, lest you miss it altogether. What reason there was for his falling a-won-dering after this whether a deeply wounded heart might be soothed and healed by such a scene, it would be difficult to explain. . . .

It is perhaps because, like many spirits of the same stock, he had in his composition a lurking principle of asceticism to whose authority he had ever paid an unques-tioning respect, that he now felt all the vehemence of rebellion. To renounce—to renounce again—to renounce forever—was this all that youth and longing and resolve were meant for? Was experience to be muffled and muti-lated, like an indecent picture? Was a man to sit and deliberately condemn his future to be the blank memory of a regret, rather than the long reverberation of a joy? Sacrifice? The word was a trap for minds muddled by fear, an ignoble refuge of weakness. To insist now seemed not to dare, but simply to be, to live on possible terms. (III, 184–85)

The phrases "simply to be, to live on possible terms" are the key, and at once James introduces his artist and his woman who are his example of those who accept "the unperverted reality of things" and "grasp frankly at experience." Longmore, however, deliberately begins to confuse the situation. He asks himself as he watches the painter wait for his lady, "Was it his work . . . that made him so happy? Was a strong talent the best thing in the world? . . . Longmore sat brooding and asking himself whether it was better to cultivate an art than to cultivate a passion. Before he had answered the question the painter had grown tired of waiting" (III, 186). The truth is pointed at by the artist's ironic action, ironic in light of what Longmore is thinking. There is no conflict between art and passion as choices in life; *both* must exist, and the mature man will sense the necessity of each, even if they are only reconciled with extreme difficulty. James also shows these two concepts existing in the artist's woman: "She was graceful, she was charming, she had an air of decision and yet of sweetness, and it seemed to Longmore that a young artist would work none the worse for having her seated at his side, reading Chénier's iambics" (III, 187). The passages seem to build *for the reader* a clear case: art and life's passion can live together. The confusion comes in Longmore's mind.

> Every now and then the episode of the happy young painter and the charming woman who had given up a great many things for him rose vividly in his mind, and seemed to mock his moral unrest like some obtrusive vision of unattainable bliss.
>
> The landlady's gossip cast no shadow on its brightness; her voice seemed that of the vulgar chorus of the uninitiated, which stands always ready with its gross prose rendering of the inspired passages in human action. Was it possible a man could take *that* from a woman,—take all that lent lightness to that other woman's footstep and intensity to her glance,—and not give her the absolute certainty of a devotion as unalterable as the process of the sun? Was it possible that such a rapturous union had the seeds of trouble,—that the charm of such a perfect accord could be broken by anything but death? Longmore felt an immense desire to cry out a thousand times "No!" for it seemed to him at last that he was somehow spiritually the same as the young painter, and that the latter's companion had the soul of Euphemia de Mauves. (III, 189–90)

Right after this passage Longmore has his dream in which James shows how Longmore is different from the artist. The artist can easily take from his woman without giving anything so "absolute" and "unalterable" as Longmore in his childish and romantic idealism must assume. The woman also sees the situation for what it is, but Longmore has, actually, seen nothing realistically. He has created another way out for himself. He still refuses to act as a man should act, as the artist acts. For the artist there is no impossible conflict between talent and passion, art and life. They and their conflict are the inevitable necessities of our existence: it is life that feeds talent and art, and it is passion—the "vigorous natural life" that suggests "very little that was transcendental, had very little to say about renunciation,—nothing at all about spiritual zeal"—that feeds life. Longmore has no passion, no life, no art. He is the emasculated American male held up to scorn.

It is important to see how James embodies this necessary conflict between life and art in the construction of the scene. The setting is idealistic—too artistically constructed to be real—and in it exist the artist and his woman in the perfect relationship, too perfect. As the innkeeper suggests, this relationship will not last, just as this ideal scene will not last forever. Nothing, obviously, does; winter always comes. There is only conflict in this realization for the man of fantasy; there is no conflict for the man of true feeling. What the sensitive man does is not absolute but is subject to the inevitable elements of our complex life; and in James's morality, the fine man is the one who responds to the fullest actualities of a situation, not to an idealistic code that has no relevance to reality.

It is Madame de Mauves who personifies the intransigent principle of morality. She is a tightly controlled and excessively romantic woman. As a young girl in a convent in Paris, Euphemia is befriended by a French girl in order to be introduced to this friend's brother, the Baron de Mauves. From the start the de Mauves family intends to arrange a marriage. On Euphemia's first visit to the family estate, the grandmother recognizes her American purity and naïveté, which are the means the de Mauves family will shrewdly use to deceive her and get her money for the preservation of their family. As the grandmother says to her, " 'It's easy to see that you're not one of us. I don't know whether you're better, but you seem to me to listen to the murmur of your own young spirit, rather than to the voice from behind the confessional or to the whisper of opportunity' " (III, 133). Whether better or worse, her difference from the de Mauves family is in her being a sensitive American, and as a sensitive American she views Europe romantically.

Euphemia Cleve naïvely suffers, as does Clement Searle, another passionate pilgrim, from an absence of the romantic in her native environment and from an acutely deprived sensitivity that makes her overestimate the romantic in Europe. She does not go insane from her contact with Europe as Searle does; James has succeeded here in better structuring his ideas. She simply imagines, as James carefully points out (III, 129–30), a romance that has no relationship to reality, and blinded by this romantic image of Europe, she marries the French baron of her dreams. She is pure, simple, direct, and absolute, without any of the shades of his evil past. She does not let reality affect her resolve. When such a nature is injured, when its conscience is righteously aroused, it can become a powerfully strong and intolerant mechanism. She will not, like the French, let reality push her into skepticism and easy cynicism. She ignores reality and retreats into idealistic renunciation and ends with nothing but a dutiful, magnificent, cold conscience. As she says to Longmore:

> "Philosophy?" she said. "I have none. Thank Heaven!" she cried, with vehemence, "I have none. I believe, Mr. Longmore," she added in a moment, "that I have nothing

on earth but a conscience,—it's a good time to tell you so, —nothing but a dogged, clinging, inexpugnable conscience. Does that prove me to be indeed of your faith and race, and have you one for which you can say as much? I don't say it in vanity, for I believe that if my conscience will prevent me from doing anything very base, it will effectually prevent me from doing anything very fine." (III, 171)

She says right after this, in response to Longmore: " 'Don't laugh at your conscience . . . that's the only blasphemy I know' " (III, 172).

Madame de Mauves is without the nuances of light and color that she imagines she sees everywhere in Europe. She is emotionally inflexible and unrealistic. Her husband, who in another way is strikingly limited, sees her limitations. He says to Longmore, " 'If Madame de Mauves too would travel for a couple of months, it would do her good. It would enlarge her horizon . . . it would show her that one may bend a trifle without breaking' " (III, 160). Madame de Mauves sees no possibility for bending at all.

"I hate tragedy," she once said to him; "I have a really pusillanimous dread of moral suffering. I believe that—without base concessions—there is always some way of escaping from it. I had almost rather never smile all my life than have a single violent explosion of grief." She lived evidently in nervous apprehension of being fatally convinced,—of seeing to the end of her deception. (III, 153)

She is not without awareness of herself, and James does admire the quality if not the effect of her resolve. She admits she is romantic, that life is "hard prose" (III, 169) in Europe as well as America, and that her foolish, young illusions have led her to where she is, but she stubbornly refuses to renounce her beliefs for those she considers base, even though her beliefs also entail the denial of any life for herself.

What the reader is led to wonder is if Euphemia, for all her moral grandeur, is not perhaps approachable? The point is *not* conclusive in the tale, only suggested by her general responsiveness to Longmore and refusal to send him away until she has learned of Madame Clairin's proposition. The point is also suggested by the parallel to the artist and his lady, which Longmore makes right before his dream. Perhaps in Euphemia the element of romance is so strong that, properly approached, she could have an affair with Longmore. He must, however, attempt this affair in a way that fulfills her romantic ideal. Once her husband and his sister have entered, it is too late for this proud woman. The idea is only suggested in the tale, but if this suggestion seems substantial, it shows James dealing with the subtle innuendoes of a mind that wants merely to appear pure in order to imagine itself so; and the criticism of Euphemia and her American morality must then become, in light of her later actions, even more devastating. She is not just injured and self-righteous; she is then deliberately and hypocritically playing the role of the martyr.

In contrast to her is the Baron de Mauves, the cynical, materialistic Frenchman who marries for money and then assumes his wife will expect him to take a mistress. We are never in any doubt about his intentions. He cannot at first conceive of his wife's idealistic perfection, her romantic, dutiful American disposition, except as a charming means to his ends. He finally admires her grandeur and he does, it is indicated, repent. The question then becomes one of whose background better prepares him for what exists. Euphemia cannot conceive of such a husband, nor conceive of the Baron seeing what she is and repenting. He does not expect such a wife, but finally sees the beauty in her, repents his follies, and falls in love with her. The French milieu breeds its corruption, but also its own form of renewal, in terms of its imaginative awareness of the possibilities of life; the American seed in Europe produces a straighter, purer, but a less flexible and resilient plant.

Such a comparison does not exhaust the possibilities. Madame de Mauves, in her American resolution to create her vision, is a type of romantic artist of life; the Baron is more of a crude, heavy vulgarian. Longmore, to further the national perspective, stands between the two, trying, as best he can, to see all he can. Madame Clairin in her decadence represents a European vulgarity that insists upon maintaining its own code of behavior as rigid as Euphemia's.[6] The artist seems to be the ideal; he is the only one who does not prescribe action but accepts reality. It is his artistic vision and freedom, not his nationality, that condition his view of life.

It is also important for a reader to see that the story is deliberately romantic. Once James conceives of his examination of character in international terms, he has to deal with the question of romance, for the international situation is in part the contrast between the ideally romantic and the actual. The element of romance in the international situation becomes too heavy in *The American,* destroying the novel's realistic balance. In "Madame de Mauves" it is kept in line. There is enough suggestion of the idyllic, romantic fantasies we can conceive in our lives, but there is also criticism of our failure to see reality and truth. It is in this balance that Longmore becomes so important. We see him attempting to understand what is romance and what is reality, and it is what we see *more* than he that is the degree of truth that James expects us to accept as the significant moral distinction of the tale. We must be more than just in awe of Madame de Mauves. To be only in awe is to be unaware. We must see her in the fullness of our imaginative power. We must do the same with the Baron. Our consciousness must grow beyond Longmore's until it is truly international, and only as it is this intangible quality is our understanding great and our vision of the story real. Once James conceives of his examination of character in the international mold, and the structure is so formed, we as readers are then in the same contrasting position and must give our fullest awareness to all the various, complex elements of his vision. If we do not do this, we become less than his intention demands.

The international theme of "Madame de Mauves" is reflected primarily in the contrasts between Euphemia, her husband, his family, and Longmore. It is important to examine with it *Roderick Hudson,* written shortly after this tale, for here James develops the theme on a broader and more important canvas.[7] In *Roderick Hudson* the international theme is set in the contrasts between Northampton, Massachusetts, and Rome; Mary Garland and Christina Light; the new and the old. It also comes, as the theme is refined, in the contrast between the artist, Roderick Hudson, and his mentor, Rowland Mallet, and the conflict they represent between art and life. Roderick and Rowland—their names are different but too similar not to be confused—represent two sides of one personality. Together they form a balance in character that does not seem to be possible in reality. As the novel is examined, it appears that each of the major characters represents a certain attempt at this balance, but this balance is subtle—perhaps, in its complexity, beyond our actual creation.

The correlation between the international theme and the life of the artist is suggested in "Madame de Mauves" and developed in *Roderick Hudson.* Only the "artist" is fully free to see, to feel and experience, and then to express himself effectively. As pointed out in the discussion of "Madame de Mauves," it is not the young artist who is confused by life, only the inadequate Long-more who is tied to his American limitations. The point is made by James as early as 1868 in "The Story of a Masterpiece" where only the artist Baxter can see fully and express his vision, not the inadequate Lennox, who must destroy his fiancée's portrait that shows in art too much of life. The artist becomes for James the individual who can most effectively fulfill the true international vision because he sees all aspects of life, responds to them, and can make them effective in his life and art. James considers someone like Maggie Verver an artist of life, as much an artist as any writer or painter. That he frequently makes this artist an American is, it would seem, because of the American's opportunity to choose freely the broad view that the more traditional European cannot. This attitude toward Americans does not, obviously, exclude the possibility of the European becoming such an artist of life. In *The Europeans* Felix, who is a painter and proper Bohemian, is an example, as is the young painter in "Madame de Mauves." James, in shaping his international vision, could not be so parochial as to exclude the European, any more than he could insist upon one type of art or one type of artist. It is only that the conditions of being American for James seem to lead more easily to the international vision.

To be an artist is for James not an evasion of life, but a means to retaining as much life as possible. He speaks at one point in *The Tragic Muse* of what "any artistic performance requires and that all, whatever the instrument, require in exactly the same degree," and what they require is "the perfect presence of mind, unconfused, unhurried by emotion . . . the application, in other words, clear and calculated, crystal-firm as it were, of the idea conceived in the glow of experience, of suffering, of joy." [8] The danger is that one might not be able to balance effectively the contrasts in the ambiguities of character. That possibility does not preclude, however, the validity of the attempt any more than it precludes the endlessly present conflict in the artist to keep a balance. The ambivalence and conflict are built into the human character. James's later tales of artists, "The Author of Beltraffio" and "The Lesson of the Master," which are not international tales, still show him painfully conscious of the necessity of keeping a balance as a writer between the demands of art—its duties and disciplines—and the experiences of life. Isabel Archer and Milly Theale are different women with different concerns, but what they are unable to do is to achieve a life that effectively contains all that they see as possible. The weakness of Kate Croy is vividly seen because she uses obviously evil means, but she is not without a brilliant consciousness and she is attempting in the most vibrant way to construct life artistically. Her vitality must be recognized as that which Milly lacks, for all our admiration for what Milly does achieve in her death. In *The Golden Bowl* Maggie Verver faces Charlotte Stant with the will to make life work *and* with the artistic finesse to carry through her will, which is what Milly Theale lacks in her contact with Kate. The conflict in *The Tragic Muse* and in *The Princess Casamassima*, which are not international novels, is in this attempt to balance art and life in order to obtain the fullest vision, experience, and control possible. Gabriel Nash, in one discussion with his friend Nick Dormer in *The Tragic Muse*, explains the relationship between art, life, and control. Nash and Dormer seem to represent two sides of the human character—the aesthetic and the moral—and between them they create a balance.

"Don't you recognize in *any* degree the elevated idea of duty?" . . .

"Do I gather that you yourself recognize obligations of the order you allude to?" asked Nick.

"Do you 'gather'?" Nash stared. "Why, aren't they the

very flame of my faith, the burden of my song?"

"My dear fellow, duty is doing, and I inferred that you think rather poorly of doing—that it spoils one's style."

"Doing wrong, assuredly."

"But what do you call right? What's your canon of certainty there?"

"The conscience that's in us—that charming, conversible, infinite thing, the intensest thing we know. But you must treat the oracle civilly if you wish to make it speak. You mustn't stride into the temple in muddy jack-boots, with your hat on your head, as the Puritan troopers tramped into the dear old abbeys. One must do one's best to find out the right, and your criminality appears to be that you have not taken common trouble."

"I hadn't you to ask," smiled Nick. "But duty strikes me as doing *something*. If you are too afraid it may be the wrong thing, you may let everything go."

"Being is doing, and if doing is duty, being is duty. Do you follow?"

"At a great distance."

"To be what one *may* be, really and efficaciously," Nash went on, "to feel it and understand it, to accept it, adopt it, embrace it—that's conduct, that's life."

"And suppose one's a brute or an ass, where's the efficacy?"

"In one's very want of intelligence. In such cases one is out of it—the question doesn't exist; one simply becomes a part of the duty of others. The brute, the ass, neither feels, nor understands, nor accepts, nor adopts. Those fine processes in themselves classify us. They educate, they exalt, they preserve; so that, to profit by them, we must be as perceptive as we can. We must recognize our particular form, the instrument that each of us—each of us who carries anything—carries in his being. Mastering this instrument, learning to play it in perfection—that's what I call duty, what I call conduct, what I call success." [9]

Roderick Hudson is James's earliest attempt to express this complex control of life and art in the international structure. A rich American, Rowland Mallet, takes Roderick Hudson from Northampton, Massachusetts, to Rome in order to submit him to the world of art. Rowland thinks the young American sculptor will thrive in such a world and fulfill his promise, and it is this experience Rowland wants to be a part of and to observe. Roderick does come alive and in a startling way, but Europe's power, in the form of a beautiful woman, half American, half European, is too much for him. He loses his past, his sense of himself, his talent, and finally his life in a mountain accident as he returns from visiting this now-married woman with whom he is hopelessly infatuated.

Roderick can be described as someone who plunges in over his head. His relationship with Christina Light is passionate and profound. She is the *human* embodiment of the complex European civilization that Rome represents. With her the area of the possible is enlarged, and it is to Roderick's credit that he sees and appreciates this power of hers. She is not free to marry him. She must do what she does not truly want to do and marry nobility and money. Roderick is tied to the past—to his widowed mother and his fiancée, Mary Garland. It is impossible for him to maintain the balance between the forces of life and the disciplines of his art. He has everything for success in life *except* what his counterpart Rowland has: order and control; the ability to structure the meaning. On the other hand, Rowland is without Roderick's genius and his passionate commitment.

The conflict in the novel is between art and life and the great demands of each. This conflict is first expressed in the contrast between America and Europe. In Northampton it is the innocence and renunciation of the materialistic life that produce Roderick's art but, if he were to remain, would restrict it, and in Rome it is art and passion that give him freedom but also destroy with excess. Because of the life she must lead, Christina Light is herself, as she says, " 'corrupt, corruptible, corruption.' " [10] She is because she is forced to give so much of the European side of life: " 'There's nothing I can't imagine! That's my trouble.' " [11] This side is evil to the degree that it does not renounce excess. It is powerful to the degree that it does not deny art and life.

Roderick is a genius without the ability to sustain the balance between art and life that would permit him to create and, eventually, to live. He is the American genius: free, open, natural—complete except in his fatal lack of control and order. Roderick's first major statue, done in Northampton, is of a young man, his head thrown back, self-confidently drinking from a gourd: "Its beauty was the beauty of natural movement." [12] The figure is described by Roderick himself as representing youth, innocence, health, strength, and curiosity. Like a child, the figure appears self-assured to the point of being only self-interested. The cup he drinks is knowledge, pleasure, experience; and Roderick, in reply to Rowland's question about how deeply he is drinking, says, " 'Aye, poor fellow, he's thirsty!' " [13] This first sculpture is a symbol for Roderick, the American artist, a combination of exciting genius and unconscious weakness. He must drink of Europe—there is no choice—and he must drink in his own way. The question is, what will happen? James says the inevitable, and he makes the observation several times: that as genius comes uncalled, so does whatever happens to this genius. Roderick says of himself:

> "There are all kinds of indefinable currents moving to and fro between one's will and one's inclinations. People talk as if the two things were essentially distinct; on different sides of one's organism, like the heart and the liver. Mine, I know, are much nearer together. It all depends upon circumstances. I believe there is a certain group of circumstances possible for every man, in which his will is destined to snap like a dry twig." [14]

Rowland writes to his cousin in Northampton about Roderick:

> He is the most extraordinary being, the strangest mixture of qualities. I don't understand so much force going with so much weakness—such a brilliant gift being subject to such lapses. The poor fellow is incomplete, and it is really not his own fault; Nature has given him the faculty out of hand and bidden him be hanged with it. I never knew a man harder to advise or assist, if he is not in the mood for listening. I suppose there is some key or other to his character, but I try in vain to find it; and yet I can't believe that Providence is so cruel as to have turned the lock and thrown the key away.[15]

The potentiality is great, but the result, given the conditions, is only what it must be. This point is particularly well made in the novel as the other characters contrast in their own fated strengths and weaknesses with Roderick—especially Rowland, who has little but has just what Roderick needs. Rowland's consciousness sees this and can do nothing about it. None of the characters has Roderick's genius, which they all recognize. Only Christina has a certain greatness in seeing what is in life, although she knows she is completely destructive of life. All of them are fated to be less than Roderick, but to have degrees of order that he lacks. The power of fate in the novel is effectively shown through the character of Mary Garland, Roderick's fiancée. Once submitted to Rome she begins to understand its qualities. She becomes someone who might be capable of giving order and life to Roderick if only it were possible for him not to be so enraptured with Christina and Europe. Mary has a long conversation with Rowland in which she shows how sensitively her nature is attempting to balance the elements of the international vision, but Roderick can now no more love her than she can love Rowland, who has fallen in love with Mary.

"I'm overwhelmed. Here in a single hour, everything is changed. It is as if a wall in my mind had been knocked down at a stroke. Before me lies an immense new world, and it makes the old one, the poor little narrow, familiar one I have always known, seem pitiful."

"But you didn't come to Rome to keep your eyes fastened on that narrow little world. Forget it, turn your back on it, and enjoy all this." . . .

"To enjoy, as you say, as these things demand of one to enjoy them, is to break with one's past. And breaking is a pain!"

"Don't mind the pain, and it will cease to trouble you. Enjoy, enjoy; it's your duty. Yours especially!" . . .

She looked away from him for some moments, down the gorgeous vista of the great church. "But what you say," she said at last, "means *change!*"

"Change for the better!" cried Rowland.

"How can one tell? As one stands, one knows the worst. It seems to me very frightful to develop," she added, with her complete smile.

"One is in for it in one way or another, and one might as well do it with a good grace as with a bad! Since one can't escape life, it is better to take it by the hand."

"Is *this* what you call life?" she asked.

"What do you mean by 'this'?"

"Saint Peter's—all this splendor, all Rome—pictures, ruins, statues, beggars, monks."

"It's not all of it, but it's a large part of it. All these things are impregnated with life; they are the fruits of an old and complex civilization." [16]

What Roderick does not see—or perhaps because of what he is he *cannot* see—is what Mary Garland and the artist in "Madame de Mauves" seem to understand. Nature is changing *and* constant; it is free and spontaneous, but not without a necessary order and structure. The true artist must know that this ambivalence in nature also exists in the human being and accept the conflicting elements, seeking what order he can create. If

Roderick is a victim of his fate, as James seems to suggest, he is the pathetic and magnificent failure of a great talent that could not adjust to this view of life. Rowland is the order without the commitment of passion. For all his talk to Mary Garland, he can never make her love him. Only a few people can transcend the limitations of existence and artistically deal with experience in the broadest possible context while still maintaining a balance and an order. To do so is to be the artist of life. To go too far as Roderick does is beyond his choice. To fail to go out is Rowland's condition. Neither is to be condemned, only to be seen as failing to achieve as much as is possible.

James seems to suggest in *Roderick Hudson* that as man must transcend the conditions of life presented to him, he must also accept the conditions of what he is. An inevitable dilemma then results: it is painful to be less than what seems possible, but more destructive and meaningless to try to be what one is not. In *The Portrait of a Lady* James suggests his attitude toward this dilemma in the character of Isabel Archer. She works only within the conditions of what she is, and her choices, right or wrong, are those of a creature "affronting her destiny," as he says of her. She is, to use Gabriel Nash's terms, "doing" her duty by "mastering" the instrument of her fate. It is those who make this confrontation with awareness, such as Isabel, Milly Theale, and Maggie Verver, whom James admires, for all their failure, and those who do not whom he finds insignificant. It is for this reason that Roderick has our admiration even though we see so clearly—as he does—his failure. It is why we sympathize with rather than judge Madame de Mauves. In the magnificent limitation of what she is, she has no other choice of action. It is their potential awareness of another choice not taken that makes Rowland and Longmore less sympathetic to us. Seldom is one condemned in James's vision; people are seen only for what they are.

In James's view of life, structured upon his international vision, it is the true artists who come closest to the ideal that the rest of us seek, if we are aware, or ignore completely in our narrowness. James seems to suggest that all of us can make ourselves more aware, more the artist, but the true artistic genius is fated to be such. We can observe this artist, understand him, but there is nothing that can make us an artist if we ourselves do not have the genius. We can only become the fine consciousness of a fate that is not ours to share. In many senses it can be said that we share in the consciousness and fate of James's limited narrators, and that is why they are for James—and for us—the real subject of this fiction.

During this same period from 1873 to 1875, James wrote several other tales, but only one of these attempts to consider the complex themes that are found in "Madame de Mauves" and developed in *Roderick Hudson*. The other tales of this period are only illustrative of certain ideas that James is developing. For instance, "The Last of the Valerii" (1874) and "Adina" (1874) are stories of the dark past of Italy, a past that for James consists of suspicion, horror, and paganism. The tales have a certain strange fascination, but they are slight in content and not distinctive in style. They point out James's peculiar impression of how this Italian past still exists in the present. It is an impression that seems close to Hawthorne's in *The Marble Faun*, and for all its dark interest and insight, it is a limited impression.

"The Madonna of the Future" (1873) and "The Sweetheart of M. Briseux" (1873) are tales about artists. "The Madonna of the Future" is reprinted in the New York Edition, and the comments James made in his Preface about "A Passionate Pilgrim" also apply to it: the tale's interest for James is personal and he makes no claim for its merit beyond this interest. "The Madonna of the Future" has been consistently overestimated, along with "A Passionate Pilgrim," because of James's personal interest and the possible autobiographical importance. In "The Madonna of the Future" James as a young writer is concerned with the possibility that he will not be able to continue to write effectively, that he has the vision of his art only in his mind and will not be able to execute works as the less idealistic artist can more easily do. Although he sets the tale in an international context, James makes the artist in "The Madonna of the Future" like Clement Searle in "A Passionate Pilgrim," too absurd to be representative and too romantic to be real. The sane and reasonable narrator James creates to tell the story does not keep the balance of this tale any more than such a narrator does in "A Passionate Pilgrim."

The other artist tale, which has received less attention, is "The Sweetheart of M. Briseux." In it a woman relates how, many years ago, a now-famous artist had painted her portrait. She has not seen this artist again, but her portrait was his first great work; the portrait also resulted in the end of her engagement to another artist, a man of little sensitivity whom she did not love. The woman reveals a deeply sensitive nature as she relates how she responded to the power of the great artist. The tale has some connection with "The Story of a Masterpiece" for it shows art revealing truth, forcing the real to the surface, but it is in no way intended to be as serious or as subtle a tale as "The Story of a Masterpiece." "The Sweetheart of M. Briseux" is told as a story-within-a-story, making it slow to start, but it is written with ease and humor.

It has been pointed out that "Professor Fargo" (1874) is of interest because it suggests certain elements in a later novel: the world of spiritualists and materialists found in *The Bostonians*.[17] The ugliness of this world is powerfully portrayed in the tale and is found again in the parents of Verena Tarrant and the atmosphere of corruption they carry. For this reason the tale is curious as an atypical Jamesian study of one aspect of America. It is also unusual in that the last part of the tale is set in New York City and conveys some of the crassness and poverty of that city seen at its worst. James uses the falseness of spiritualism as a contrast with true intellectualism and he embodies these concepts in the vulgar Professor Fargo and a mild old mathematician who has been reduced to working as a partner with Fargo in his stage performances. The mathematician is a genius, but he is at the mercy of his materialistic society, represented at its worst in Fargo's spiritualism. Fargo finally takes from the old man his brilliant deaf-and-dumb daughter, to use in his act. The symbolic references to American life are obvious: intellect, genius, sensitivity lose all they possess to hypocrisy and materialism in a land that cannot see and does not value quality. The loss of the daughter to Fargo suggests that the future will be worse: as brilliant and sensitive as she is, she is deaf to what Fargo really wants to do to her quality. As the story ends, the old man goes into an institution.

"Eugene Pickering" (1874) is the one tale in the group that has elements similar to those in "Madame de Mauves" and *Roderick Hudson*. A German lady, a novelist, as responsive and intelligent as Christina Light, encounters Eugene Pickering, an inexperienced American who combines Longmore's propriety and Roderick Hudson's passion. She sees in him an unusual experience with a brilliant and innocent American man, and he finds in her his grand encounter with the world and love. She tires first of him, as might be expected, but he has learned something of the ways of the world. The result is not depressing. Eugene soon recovers from his spell of

Europe to marry an American girl—oddly enough, one living in Smyrna.

The tale is written with great charm and lightness. Two quotations suggest its sensitive perceptions and also indicate how James is expressing here some of the same ideas that he is concerned with in writing "Madame de Mauves" and *Roderick Hudson*. The first quotation is spoken by Eugene as he defines his sudden realization and fear of life—in images of water and plunging similar to those found in Longmore's dream. The second is by the German lady. Her character and this quotation also prefigure the character of Eugenia in *The Europeans*.

"I've lived more in the past six weeks than in all the years that preceded them. I'm filled with this feverish sense of liberation; it keeps rising to my head like the fumes of strong wine. I find I'm an active, sentient, intelligent creature, with desires, with passions, with possible convictions,—even with what I never dreamed of, a possible will of my own! I find there is a world to know, a life to lead, men and women to form a thousand relations with. It all lies there like a great surging sea, where we must plunge and dive and feel the breeze and breast the waves. I stand shivering here on the brink, staring, longing, wondering, charmed by the smell of the brine and yet afraid of the water. The world beckons and smiles and calls, but a nameless influence from the past, that I can neither wholly obey nor wholly resist, seems to hold me back. I'm full of impulses, but, somehow, I'm not full of strength. Life seems inspiring at certain moments, but it seems terrible and unsafe; and I ask myself why I should wantonly measure myself with merciless forces, when I have learned so well how to stand aside and let them pass. . . . I don't know whether you are laughing at my trepidation or at what possibly strikes you as my depravity. I doubt," he went on gravely, "whether I have an inclination toward wrong-doing; if I have, I'm sure I sha'n't prosper in it. I honestly believe I may safely take out a license to amuse myself. But it isn't that I think of, any more than I dream of playing with suffering. Pleasure and pain are empty words to me; what I long for is knowledge,—some other knowledge than comes to us in formal, colorless, impersonal precept. You would understand all this better if you could breathe for an hour the musty indoor atmosphere in which I have always lived. To break a window and let in light and air,—I feel as if at last I must *act!*" (III, 310–11)

"No matter, no matter!" she cried, "I should like to see the country which produced that wonderful young man. I think of it as a sort of Arcadia,—a land of the golden age. He's so delightfully innocent! In this stupid old Germany, if a young man is innocent, he's a fool; he has no brains; he's not a bit interesting. But Mr Pickering says the most näif things, and after I have laughed five minutes at their simplicity, it suddenly occurs to me that they are very wise, and I think them over for a week. True!" she went on, nodding at him. "I call them inspired solecisms, and I treasure them up. Remember that when I next laugh at you!" (III, 332)

"Benvolio" (1875), the last of these tales, is James's only deliberate allegory, and one must avoid reading too much of James's life into the flat pattern of this long and obvious tale. Benvolio is a young poet of immense talent and personal charm who divides his life between the elegant social world of the Countess and the quiet, secluded garden of Scholastica. The conflict in him is symbolized by his two rooms: his elaborately decorated sitting room looks out to the street and is filled with friends, and the sparse and monastic bedroom where he writes looks out on a secluded garden. Such a contrast and division is necessary for Benvolio. When Scholastica leaves, at the Countess's instigation, Benvolio's spirits begin to wane. Finally he says to the Countess: " 'Don't you see . . . can't you imagine, that I cared for you only by contrast? You took the trouble to kill the contrast, and with it you killed everything else. For a constancy I prefer *this!*' And he tapped his poetic brow. He never saw the Countess again" (III, 401). He eventually finds Scholastica and begins to write once more, "only, many people said that his poetry had become dismally dull" (III, 401). The artist needs the contrasts of life in some balance to create art; "a poet, in order to do full justice to his poetic genius and temperament, must achieve a balance between the world and the closet, for both are indispensable to the proper fruition of his genius." [18]

James wrote "Benvolio" during the months he spent in New York City in 1875. It was the only tale he wrote at that time, although he published innumerable reviews in his attempt to live off the American literary market place. The experience was unsatisfactory, and it was immediately after this period that James decided to settle permanently in Europe. In "Benvolio" James presents directly the two irreconcilable elements of any sensitive character: the desire to live life fully, but also to articulate and define life in some effective way. For certain artists the two problems are one—their life is their art. James then sees these artists as fighting for their life against corrupting forces, such as Ralph Touchett and Milly Theale must do. For other artists the conflict is directly between life and the creation of art, as in the conflict of *Roderick Hudson* and "The Lesson of the Master." In either case art is what the individual finally aspires to because it is the subtlest embodiment of life open to man. What "Benvolio" shows more blatantly than any other work is that although this conflict is irreconcilable and painful, it is also necessary, for to create well one must live well and in the quality of one will come the art of the other.

What James has moved to by the time he finishes "Benvolio" is a conception of life based upon the quality of the artistic imagination. The artist and the internationalist—who is for James the artist of life—see man as unbound by the limitations of any position and always moving toward the fullest realization of what the mind's eye can see. Their fate is to try to transcend the limited fate of others. In attempting to achieve the greatest potentialities of life through the greatest vision of life, they see that only *in* conscious artistic creation can man hope to achieve some of what he sees as possible. Art, in its broadest sense, becomes life, becomes the means of trying to transcend the limitations of life.

4

The Determined Artist: 1876–1880

When Henry James wrote to his mother on March 26, 1870, from England, he devoted the letter to Minny Temple, his cousin, who had just died of a prolonged lung illness.[1] In this letter James lets go of his usual reserve: "It is no surprise to me to find that I felt for her an affection as deep as the foundations of my being, for I always knew it; but I now become sensible how her image, softened and sweetened by suffering and sitting patient and yet expectant, so far away from the great world with which so many of her old dreams and impulses were associated, has operated in my mind as a gentle incentive to action and enterprise."[2] Near the end of his letter James comments on the peculiar and powerful quality of this woman for whom life held such endless but impossible potential.

> On the dramatic fitness—as one may call it—of her early death it seems almost idle to dwell. No one who ever knew her can have failed to look at her future as a sadly insoluble problem—and we almost all had imagination enough to say, to murmur at least, that life—poor narrow life—contained no place for her. How all her conduct and character seem to have pointed to this conclusion—how profoundly inconsequential, in her history, continued life would have been![3]

The comment is strange: it seems to indicate that the imaginative possibilities of Minny's life are so much greater than the realistic possibilities that had she lived, her life could only have been less. James no doubt is considering the conflict between her desire for life and her chronic poor health, but he is also looking at the quality of the mind that is able to see so much more in life than life can actually contain. The potentialities of experience are most fully realized in the imagination, and it is only the great imagination that can see and conceive of the fullest potentialities in life.

This view of life is inevitably tragic as it must lead to failure and to unrealized possibilities; no matter how great the attempt, there will always be something not achieved. This condition is particularly acute for the artist who constantly works with the inevitable conflicts between imaginative possibility and reality. His choice of art as life is not necessarily less meaningful, if well experienced, than any other choice, but the inevitable gap between the possible and the actual—the envisioned and the realized—is greater for the artist than it is for anyone else. He has to contend with the inevitable human tragedy all of us face, but he must also contend with his own failure to realize fully this vision of tragedy in his art. There is, however, no other choice for the committed artist. "It is art that *makes* life, makes interest, makes importance . . . and I know of no substitute whatever for the force and beauty of its process." [4]

As one approaches James's first major period—when he wrote "Daisy Miller," "An International Episode," *The Europeans*, *Washington Square*, and *The Portrait of a Lady*—one can see his fine handling of this inevitable conflict between the possible and the actual.[5] The great interest here is in the precision of his observation and the lucidity of his style. James will in his later work attempt much more, but he will seldom achieve so much perfection in execution as he does at this time. This comparison is not meant to diminish the quality of the later works, nor it is meant to ignore the novels of the 1880's that continue what is started in the late 1870's, particularly *The Bostonians* and *The Reverberator*; it is only to suggest the special nature of this first period. The writing of the early period is more alive, less self-conscious, less deliberately constructed for effect. One admires the exactness of what is seen at this point even though it is less than what he later attempts to see. The inevitable tragedy of life and art—the conflict between what is seen and achieved—is slighter here, for although what is attempted is less, the achievement is firmer.

Most of the tales of the period from 1876 to 1880 are well written; only four of the ten are inferior work. Even three of these four should be commented on briefly before moving to the better tales, as these three—"Crawford's Consistency" (1876), "The Ghostly Rental" (1876), and "Longstaff's Marriage" (1878)—have certain unusual and even fascinating elements that are peculiar to James. "Crawford's Consistency" is a melodrama of marriage: a mild, respectable man, jilted by an upper-class woman, takes on the rebound a lower-class wife. She starts to drink and literally tries to kill him after he has lost his money, but he remains consistent to her. The pace of the tale is excellent, and the drama even becomes melodramatic as it exposes through marriage the fatuous and materialistic values of society and reveals in a simplistic moral statement the quality of human decency. James implies that Crawford's marriage to the lower-class woman is no more blind and grotesque than the acceptable but ridiculous marriage Crawford wanted to make to the vacant society woman. Each results from the weaknesses bred into him by his society. He has not been asked to refine his intellect or his sensibilities. He has only been asked to appear to be a gentleman. Crawford refuses merely to appear a gentleman; he is one. To be a gentleman in such a society expresses a positive value that the society itself seems to lack. Crawford's consistency is in his faithfulness to his own simple, decent human reality. Crawford's wife is one of James's few characterizations of a truly uneducated and uncultured human being. James could portray this kind of person, but the simple-minded narrowness of such a character did not interest him. Although he makes the heroine of a later tale, "In the Cage," a woman without class distinction, he does make her a woman of great sensitivity and intelligence, as he portrays Brooksmith, the butler in the story of the same name. It is their exceptional qualities that make the two interesting examples of a type. Mrs. Crawford is only typical of many uneducated women; she has no quality or uniqueness. For James the type could not be the commonplace example but had to embody the ideal of a type, or the character had to be the unique exception of his class. The point is important, for it is as an ideal of a type that Daisy Miller becomes someone worth considering, for James and for us.

"The Ghostly Rental" is a lightly written, humorous, and entertaining ghost story. The narrator is a half-hearted theology student at Harvard, and the main character is an old New Englander who believes himself in the control of his daughter's ghost. The ghost is not a ghost, the daughter is not dead, but the situation is an effective means for James to explore the question of the reality of spirits and of our observation of them, and the degree to which experience must measure any judgment we make of reality. The lackadaisical theology student learns about reality from his observation of a spirit. From it and not from his studies he realizes that to observe is important and necessary, but that one must actually experience life to gain any sense of its reality; otherwise there is a greater and more painful lie between what we imagine and what actually exists. The tale could be considered in relation to *The Sacred Fount*, since the theology student soon understands that his observations, supposedly so subtle, are false—merely the work of his excited imagination. It is implied that observations not experienced are often imaginative and mysterious but usually inaccurate. At one point in the tale an old lady who never goes out but sits at her window looking at life makes a comment on the value and method of her observations. The incompleteness and the irony of her statement is borne out by the narrator's comment at the end of it and by the outcome of the story, which shows the old lady to have seen only part of reality.

> When I asked her how she had acquired her learning, she said simply—"Oh, I observe!" "Observe closely enough," she once said, "and it doesn't matter where you are. You may be in a pitch-dark closet. All you want is something to start with; one thing leads to another, and all things are mixed up. Shut me up in a dark closet and I will observe after a while, that some places in it are darker than others. After that (give me time), and I will tell you what the President of the United States is going to have for dinner." Once I paid her a compliment. "Your observation," I said, "is as fine as your needle, and your statements are as true as your stitches." (IV, 63)

The story suggests a contrast between theology, which should bring one to essences, and reality, which is supposed to be removed from the essential. This contrast is not seriously developed in a tale this slight, but James does imply that theology has lost its purpose and given itself to rationalistic Biblical criticism, and that reality has, for the student, become the pursuit of the essence of "spirits." Things are not, then, what they should be, and the point of the tale appears to be that to reach the truth, the pursuit of theology is senseless if one does not observe life, and the reality of life is fantastic if it is not deeply experienced. The tale has a personal application for James. As the artist committed to a life of art, he must be continually conscious of the *potential* hollowness that can come in a life not lived, merely observed. The hollowness can exist not only in the life, but it can equally appear in the work that the artist produces. It is only by consciousness and commitment that such a failure is ever avoided.[6]

"Longstaff's Marriage" is not a good story, but a peculiar one, almost perversely interesting. A dying Englishman asks a beautiful but cold American girl—Diana by name—to marry him on his deathbed and inherit his name and property. He truly loves her, but she has no feeling, not even pity, for him; she is an arrogant, virginal beauty compared several times to the goddess Diana. The story is in part based on the myth of Diana and Endymion, for the American girl, after she leaves Longstaff to die, is deeply moved by his image and falls in love with him. He does not die and many years later they meet. Now she is ill and admits she loves him, that she is "dying of love" (IV, 238). He agrees to marry her, not for love but out of respect for her condition. After she is dead he asks, " 'Did she love me or not?' " The woman's companion replies, " 'She loved you . . . more than she believed you could now love her; and it seemed to her that, when she had had her moment of happiness, to leave you at liberty was the tenderest way she could show it!' " (IV, 242). The situation is just short of absurd, but the tale has the fascination of the strange or perverse. The love-and-death relationship is a human possibility, not one often examined, yet one that poses effectively the conflict between the mind's potential and life's actualities.

It is with the publication of "Daisy Miller" in 1878 that James achieves his first great popularity and critical

attention. The selection of incidents for the slight canvas of this tale, the lightness with which the characters
are drawn, the ease with which the entire story is written
—all show the control of the young artist. Daisy is one of
the classic figures of American literature. Like Hester
Prynne, Billy Budd, Huck, the youth in *The Red Badge
of Courage*, Gatsby, Isaac McCaslin in *The Bear*—Daisy
Miller is a finely etched study of the American character
in a particularly American pose, a minor classic that
finds a place in that small group of short works that
seems so peculiar to the American achievement, as if in
longer works we could not focus so sharply on the special
and elusive quality of the American personality.

Daisy is a classic American woman even today, a reference in criticism, an observable phenomenon in life, the
ideal of a certain type of American woman. Her tale
seems too simply conceived and written for the type of
lengthy discussion it has aroused.[7] Whether Daisy is
"good" or "bad" is almost invariably debated, but the
question is not relevant to the tale and usually leads to a
moral discussion that is personal, not Jamesian. There
are two aspects of the work, however, that condition the
way one reads the tale. Once seen, they place "Daisy
Miller" with *The Scarlet Letter, Billy Budd, Huckleberry Finn, The Red Badge of Courage, The Great
Gatsby*, and *The Bear*.

Perhaps "Daisy Miller" has not always been given this
place in classic American fiction because of James's later
and greater attempts that tend to make us ignore the
significance of "Daisy Miller." Perhaps we do not see
that the tale is mythic in the same sense that each of the
other works mentioned is mythic: Daisy embodies an
essential aspect of the American experience that transcends the immediate encounter and touches upon elements common to all of us. She is unique in being the
only one of this group of American characters who is

involved directly with the European aspect of the American experience. That the tale is mythic, not realistic, and that it embodies this essential element of our experience —the European—are two concepts that once understood make much of the controversy about this tale less significant, but the tale itself more important.

The main fault in reading "Daisy Miller" comes in considering it a story that is first, and perhaps only, concerned with a description of life. The tale is no more realistic than *Huckleberry Finn* and *The Great Gatsby*: the realism of the narrative in each of these works leads to something beyond the surface incidents. What Huck, Gatsby, and Daisy represent, what motivates them to act as they do, are the significant concerns.

Daisy is the archetype of a certain American girl—innocent and pure, free to do all she thinks proper, aware of her possibilities but unconscious of herself or her world beyond the immediate desires of her female soul: to be beautiful, to be flattering to men and flattered by them, to be protected by her suitors and successfully married to one, to become the matriarch of a prosperous home and family. She has no evil intentions, nor has she any consciousness of the evil that innocent intentions can suggest and create. For her a flirtation can only be moral, but her insensitivity to what her actions mean—as well as her insensitivity to the meaning in the action of others—is a critical indictment. The "Roman fever" she catches is worldly evil, which is pervasive, whether she knows it or not. Her inability to see what does exist and to deal responsively with it makes her a victim of this evil—innocent but no less at fault. She is not destroyed by this evil alone, but also by the indifference of Winterbourne, the ineffectual male who does not see that as an American man his responsibility is to attempt to protect Daisy from this evil that the world contains. His job is to go into the corrupt world, into the market place, to obtain the means to keep the American woman and home pure.

As is so often suggested in Twain and several of the other writers mentioned, evil in "Daisy Miller" is associated with the old world, the unregenerated land of the unregenerated man, or with those fallen and corrupted representatives of the new world. Winterbourne is a victim of Europe, having been educated there—he has a mistress although he pretends to American morality—as the members of the American colony in Rome are victims because they live there. A further suggestion, implicit in the tale's situation, is that Americans—whether like Daisy or Winterbourne—cannot escape this Europe. Europe is the past Americans carry to the new world, or the past they most seek again in Europe because it is part of them. It permeates the American experience regardless of what we try to do, as evil exists regardless of what we think. These realities must be dealt with. We must control them and shape them to our ideal. If this is not possible, we must give up our ideal or die in a hopeless conflict.

"Daisy Miller" expresses a view of the American experience similar to that found in the other classic American works. Into James's tale is built the same impossible conflict between our ideals of greatness and purity and the baser realities of life, a conflict that has intrigued the American writer. The European framework of the tale makes it no less a part of the American experience. Europe is an integral aspect of America, and a refusal to admit this fact is only an example of our persistent desire for a supposedly special innocence—an innocence our writers show us can never really exist.

"An International Episode" (1878) presents a different kind of American woman from Daisy Miller. Bessie Alden, the heroine of this tale, is not the typical American girl: she is the rare exception who still maintains her undeniably American character. Daisy Miller is not all James saw of the American female, and perhaps "An International Episode" was suggested to him by his desire to do justice to the brilliant mind and fine sensitivity he found in many American women. One can imagine James feeling the necessity of doing much more with this kind of woman. She has none of the impetuousness that limits and destroys Daisy and that one finds also in Isabel Archer. Bessie's intelligence and reserve lead tragically to Milly Theale and heroically to Maggie Verver.

The tale is a satire that starts by making its attack broadly and then by refining its insights bit by bit. The story begins with an effective description of an impossibly hot summer's day in New York City. In this heat appear two trim Englishmen. James paints with wild strokes their fastidious and precious responses to New York.

> "It seems a rum-looking place."
> "Ah, very odd, very odd," said the other, who was the clever man of the two.
> "Pity it's so beastly hot," resumed the first speaker, after a pause.
> "You know we are in a low latitude," said his friend.
> "I daresay," remarked the other.
> "I wonder," said the second speaker, presently, "if they can give one a bath."
> "I daresay not," rejoined the other.
> "Oh, I say!" cried his comrade. (IV, 243–44)

They are soon ushered out of the urban heat to the country by an American, Mr. Westgate, a businessman of talent and efficient grace who makes the money his beautiful wife spends in Newport. The American businessman knows more about the English than he states, or at least than they seem to understand.

> "I say it's cooler," pursued their host, "but everything is relative. How do you stand the heat?"

"I can't say we like it," said Lord Lambeth; "but Beaumont likes it better than I."

"Well, it won't last," Mr. Westgate very cheerfully declared; "nothing unpleasant lasts over here. It was very hot when Captain Littledale was here; he did nothing but drink sherry-cobblers. He expresses some doubt in his letter whether I shall remember him—as if I didn't remember making six sherry-cobblers for him one day, in about twenty minutes. I hope you left him well; two years having elapsed since then."

"Oh, yes, he's all right," said Lord Lambeth.

"I am always very glad to see your countrymen," Mr. Westgate pursued. "I thought it would be time some of you should be coming along. A friend of mine was saying to me only a day or two ago, 'It's time for the water-melons and the Englishmen.' "

"The Englishmen and the water-melons just now are about the same thing," Percy Beaumont observed, wiping his dripping forehead.

"Ah, well, we'll put you on ice, as we do the melons. You must go down to Newport."

"We'll go anywhere!" said Lord Lambeth.

"Yes, you want to go to Newport—that's what you want to do," Mr. Westgate affirmed. "But let's see—when did you get here?"

"Only yesterday," said Percy Beaumont.

"Ah, yes, by the 'Russia.' Where are you staying?"

"At the 'Hanover,' I think they call it."

"Pretty comfortable?" inquired Mr. Westgate.

"It seems a capital place, but I can't say we like the gnats," said Lord Lambeth.

Mr. Westgate stared and laughed. "Oh, no, of course you don't like the gnats. We shall expect you to like a good many things over here, but we shan't insist upon your liking the gnats; though certainly you'll admit that, as gnats, they are fine, eh? But you oughtn't to remain in the city." (IV, 250–51)

By the time the two arrive in Newport, it is clear that

they have met their match at the social game, although in their own good-mannered way their invincible superiority makes it impossible for them to see the quality of the Americans. The Americans are better educated, as well-bred and well-mannered, and far better traveled. Even Bessie Alden, Mrs. Westgate's sister who has seen little more than Boston, knows more, and more of the world, than Lord Lambeth. Lambeth—who is repeatedly shown to be extremely pleasant and not very bright—falls in love with her. Percy Beaumont, Lambeth's companion, fears that Bessie is trying to marry a lord and wires news of the situation to Lambeth's parents. Lambeth is immediately summoned home, to a "sick" father.

Several months later Mrs. Westgate and Bessie arrive in London. Bessie assumes they will let Lord Lambeth know of their visit, as he had asked them to do, but Mrs. Westgate tells the story of certain Americans who have been snubbed in England by the English they have entertained in America. Lord Lambeth must find out for himself that they have arrived. Eventually Lambeth meets them and begins to pay his respects. He is clearly good-natured and genuine in his intentions. It is apparent he is in love and that Bessie is intrigued, but as she knows him, she sees how little there is to know, how much more she thinks he should be than he is, or than he could ever be. His mother and sister refuse at first to pay their respects to the American ladies but finally do in an attempt to impose their will on Bessie before she visits the family estate. Their hypocrisy and crassness is made clear by their fawning gentility. The next day Bessie refuses Lord Lambeth and leaves England. It is she who has seen how little they are worth. They are only curious, and poor Lambeth, although well-intentioned and recognizing the quality in Bessie, is too insensitive to know how curiously limited he and his family are.

The story is light, even slight, and the style might at

first appear not subtle enough. The quotations given are the broadest strokes James makes, and later in the tale he is less obvious. This movement in style is deliberate, and the success of the tale is in James's still strikingly original insights conveyed by this movement and in the power and sensitivity of Bessie Alden that are suggested by the movement.

Although the Americans do not escape James's sardonic wit—Mr. Westgate is just a little too smooth, Mrs. Westgate a little too clever in her endless conversation, Bessie Alden just a little too seriously Bostonian—none errs on the side of the fools as the English do. James has incisively seen the predicament of the Americans with the English that even today is often so painfully apparent: that the sensitivity and intelligence of certain Englishmen, when they deal with the best of the Americans, is sometimes dulled by misguided assumptions. They are conditioned to judge by established class characteristics, and they assume these apply in America, when indeed they seldom do. Once out of their element, these Englishmen are lost, and without the established framework to guide them, they are quite absurd specimens. What they imagine, oddly, is far less than reality—if they would only look at it.

James wrote to his mother about this tale on January 18, 1879, suggesting the nature of his obvious yet delicately conceived satire:

> It is an entirely new sensation for them (the people here) to be (at all delicately) *ironized* and satirized, from the American point of view, and they don't at all relish it. Their conception of the normal in such a relation is that the satire should be all on their side against the Americans; and I suspect that if we were to push this a little further we would find that they are extremely sensitive. But I like them too much and feel too kindly to them to go into the satire-business or even the light-ironical in any

case in which it would wound them—even if in such a case I should see my way to it very clearly.[8]

He also wrote a long letter on March 21, 1879, in answer to an English critic, Mrs. F. H. Hill, who had been annoyed by the tale and thought it untrue and unfair. It is one of the few letters James wrote to a critic, and he somewhat overstates his case.[9] He calls Lambeth "the image of a loveable, sympathetic, excellent-natured young personage, full of good feelings and of all possible delicacies of conduct."[10] James defends the use of English slang for the "pleasure-loving 'golden-youth' section of English society,"[11] and maintains he is not examining all English manners. Such an "idea is fantastic."[12] He is adamant on the point.

> One may make figures and figures without intending generalizations—generalizations of which I have a horror. I make a couple of English ladies doing a disagreeable thing —*cela c'est vu*: excuse me!—and forthwith I find myself responsible for a representation of English manners! Nothing is my *last word* about anything—I am interminably super-subtle and analytic—and with the blessing of heaven, I shall live to make all sorts of representations of all sorts of things. It will take a much cleverer person than myself to discover my last impression—among all these things—of anything. And then, in such a matter, the bother of being an American! Trollope, Thackeray, Dickens, even [sic] with their big authoritative talents, were free to draw all sorts of unflattering English pictures, by the thousand. But if I make a single one, I am forthwith in danger of being confronted with a criminal conclusion —and sinister rumours reach me as to what I think of English society. I think more things than I can undertake to tell in 40 pages of the *Cornhill*.[13]

He states that Mrs. Westgate is "too garrulous, and, on the whole, too silly" a woman to be anything but "an ironical creation."[14] This comment seems a bit hard, but still possible. It is impossible, however, to accept completely one of his comments on Mrs. Westgate: "She is not in the least intended to throw light upon the objects she criticizes, (English life and manners &c;) she is intended to throw light on the American mind alone, and its way of taking things." [15] One can allow that she is garrulous and even silly, but she is too intentionally used not to cast some light on the English side. Here James is protesting too much. The letter to his mother indicates that he had intended to make this tale a satire of the English, one that would be sharp, although not brutal and untrue. He was aiming for the delicate balance that appears in his deliberate change in style and in Bessie Alden's character.

The ending of the tale shows Bessie's power and sensitivity and how much more she sees than either Lambeth, his mother, his sister, or Mrs. Westgate. The possibilities of life that Lambeth's imagination conceived for himself, and so in part for Bessie, were insignificant in relation to what Bessie saw. She had no choice but to refuse any relationship with him, or any relationship that his family or hers could conceive for them. From the broad strokes of Lambeth's view of New York to the delicate touches of Bessie's view of London is a great and significant distance. Her acceptance of this difference—suggested in the structure of the tale and in her character —is so complete that the primacy of her imagination is confirmed against the limitations of reality.

This confirmation of the imagined ideal is one that James will explore many times again, but with particular delicacy in *The Wings of the Dove*. The validity of such a choice must always be questioned: as R. P. Blackmur says of Catherine Sloper, the heroine of *Washington Square*, "Renunciation . . . is a piercing virtue; one seldom knows its scope, or with what hideous weakness the apparent strength of renunciation is informed." [16] The essential concern for James is not, however, in this possible psychological problem. For most Jamesian heroines there is no other choice in life but to follow what the imagination shows as the ideal. The tragedy is in the dichotomy between what one imagines and what is actually realized. This is the tragedy of Bessie Alden's decision. It is Daisy's tragedy: although she sees very little in life and certainly cannot see that corruption exists equally with the ideal, her unconscious idealism destroys her. It is the tragedy of all the American heroines James creates on the pattern of these two. Isabel Archer learns to accept the conditions of reality, although we feel in her an unconscious idealism similar to Daisy's; even at the end Isabel seems not quite to have understood the image of her mind or the reality of her world. Milly Theale understands the battle, but she has no choice— emotionally and physically she cannot meet the demands of corruption, although no one meets the final conquest of her mind, not even Kate Croy. Maggie, the magnificent, shapes reality to suit her imagination; she has Daisy Miller's determination without her innocence and Bessie Alden's subtlety without her reserve. To meet the world on its own terms and realize our imaginative possibilities, we must be as wise and wily as serpents and as gentle and subtle as doves.

"Four Meetings," a tale written in 1877 before "Daisy Miller" and "An International Episode," is better understood when seen in relation to these two later tales. This tale concerns the four encounters the narrator makes with a New England school teacher, Caroline Spencer. The narrator begins his account in an urbane, witty voice, and his holiday journey to the country home of a friend is described in such a way as to suggest his easy sophistication with many worlds, even this rural one. He is to be a trusted observer of the four encounters because he is experienced enough to artfully construct the truth from reality. He first sees Miss Spencer at a tea party in a small Puritan New England town, one confined in a heavy winter snow, and he leafs through a photograph album of Europe with her. He believes that she is so romantically and naïvely infatuated with Europe that the experience of the pictures and his descriptions are almost unbearable to her. She can only see Europe as a romantic, Byronic ideal, and her desire to go becomes "a kind of craziness" (IV, 92). He next finds her at Le Havre, seated at a café, looking at France. What she is seeing is quaint, but it is only Le Havre and not a great thing. To her it is magnificent, and she takes in each detail as it fulfills her romantic dream. One begins to sense that her "vision" might be amiss here. Equally amiss is her view of her cousin who has come to meet her: he is a red-headed young man who pretends to Byronic dress that completely convinces Miss Spencer and disgusts the narrator. He is a painter who describes everything as "nice." The third encounter is later that day. One now sees that Miss Spencer is a hopeless romantic. She has given all her money to her cousin, who is in debt, in order that he can support a "countess" who has been disowned for marrying the cousin. He will return the money when he has painted his great picture. The narrator makes clear that he has been in the world; he has seen Europe, the cousin, and Miss Spencer; and that Europe is not Le Havre, that the cousin is a crass deceiver, and that Miss Spencer is truly blind to what is going on in front of her. Without money she must now go back to America; she has remained thirteen hours in Europe.

The last view of her is most significant. It is again where we began, in her American town. She has, in the many years since the last encounter, remained here. The money has not been repaid. The cousin is dead, but the "countess" has arrived, and the narrator sees that she is nothing but a cheap Parisian. She orders Miss Spencer about and gives "French lessons" to a hopelessly stupid American admirer. Miss Spencer has removed herself to a back room that in her poverty she has still managed to arrange artfully, but there is no apparent recognition that she has "seen" anything, least of all the reality of the countess. She appears to the narrator still a romantically starved spinster, the product of a rural New England town that James flatly calls Grimwinter. She seems to have gained nothing from life; even when Europe comes to her, she apparently sees nothing.

The meaning of the tale is in part clear from the words used to describe it, for the narrative is an expression of its theme, as are the characters and their words. It is one of the few tales in which James dramatizes the outcome of the conflict between imagination and reality *and* shows the characters still living with their dreams. The countess is a reality of Europe. So is Miss Spencer a reality of America. Yet Miss Spencer's dream of Europe is a reality for her that does not include the countess. Nor, in fact, does the countess's dream of a rich and elegant America include Miss Spencer. "Four Meetings" becomes a moral fable of the madness of our imagination when it will not use and accept the elements of reality. Miss Spencer's Europe is one without evil, yet it is only the evil of Europe, in the countess, that Caroline Spencer ever really sees. Even with this evil in front of her, Miss Spencer cannot deny the reality of what she dreams. The dream is true as well. The narrator says at the start of the story:

"I understand your case," I rejoined. "You have the native American passion—the passion for the picturesque. With us, I think, it is primordial—antecedent to experience. Experience comes and only shows us something we have dreamt of." (IV, 92)

The irony is that his remark is still true at the end of the tale. What Caroline Spencer dreams of Europe is not what we are led to believe she sees in the countess; she can still believe the Europe of her dreams is the true Europe. The countess is a mistake. Of course, such an attitude is indeed "a kind of craziness," the kind we are often not able to make ourselves escape—unless we are willing to renounce our dreams or die preserving them. If we will not do either and do not give up our dream, then we must renounce reality. Such an action must seem absurd, unreal, to anyone without the dream. Whether it actually is or not is almost impossible for anyone else to say. Through the narrator James seems to imply that Miss Spencer is to be pitied for her craziness, not to be admired, yet there is a possible question in this tale similar to the one in "Daisy Miller," that there is fault in the man as well. Why didn't the narrator do something for Miss Spencer? James suggests he is interested in her, enough so to go out of his way to see her. There is just the chance of his being in love. We are, finally, not even certain of his experience, his vision of reality, his art. There is a lingering doubt; he does not know at the end how much Miss Spencer does see of the countess for he will not speak to her, and she will not say. He never knows how much she has sacrificed for her romantic "love," nor, oddly, what really is the basis of that love. Perhaps her response was not alone to the pictures, nor just to the romance of Europe. Perhaps she would sacrifice much for a fulfillment of her romantic love.[17]

The last three tales of this period were all published in 1879. By this date James had completed *The American* and *The Europeans*, and by December, 1879, he had published his study of Hawthorne. *Washington Square* was begun at the end of this year. By May or early June of 1880, he had completed the first installments of *The Portrait of a Lady*.[18] He did not publish any tales between December, 1879, and December, 1882. Since he had begun to write tales in 1864, this is his longest period without publication of a tale. He will continue to write tales; he had only written thirty-seven by 1879 and would eventually write one hundred and twelve; but this break marks the end of the apprentice years with the tales.

The last three tales are international: "The Pension Beaurepas" (1879), the account of an American family —husband, wife, and daughter—in a pension in Geneva; "The Diary of a Man of Fifty" (1879), the story of a man in Florence who once renounced love for questionable reasons and who now tries unsuccessfully to get a young man to do the same; and "A Bundle of Letters" (1879), the letters of an international group at a pension in Paris to their friends and family at home. The tales are all slight—the second is the least successful because of the diary form and the unrealistic subject matter—but all are precisely written and are fables of the complex vision of reality that the mind creates. To describe them as fables is appropriate. The tales are simply conceived and written and, although involved with a subtle question, they only suggest a simple truth: the vision of reality is as various and complex as the mind of the individual, and the finest vision—if such a judgment can ever be made—is in the mind that imaginatively allows for the greatest complexity.

"The Pension Beaurepas" is more than just the story of an American family. Like "A Bundle of Letters," it is representative of all that the international situation could mean for James. The characters, besides the narrator and the three Americans—Mr. and Mrs. Ruck and their daughter Sophy—include Mrs. Church, an expatriate American of small means and great manners, and her daughter, Aurora; M. Pigeonneau, an elderly Frenchman from Lausanne, mostly interested in female beauty, who was once six months in Paris; and the owner of the pension, Madame Beaurepas, a woman of great astuteness and few words. Balzac's *Le Père Goriot* is mentioned on the first page, as is the famous pension of that novel, and James is attempting, on a far simpler level, a similar presentation of the myriad and horrible faces of life that are contained in the little world of a modest pension. The comparison to Balzac's work can also be seen in the author's preoccupation with money and status: Mr. Ruck's business is failing in America, but his wife and daughter refuse to let him return, refuse to stop buying; Mrs. Church cannot afford to return to America and makes a great virtue of her slight means as she fastidiously demands the most for the least money. Her daughter, an American girl raised abroad, desires nothing but America in order to be free of her mother's pettiness, but Aurora has no choice: she must play the European game and be married to the highest bidder.

All of these situations are handled lightly, even humorously, and the element of desperation runs just beneath the surface. The narrator, who is a young writer, views the scene with a light, philosophical humor, is "not rich—on the contrary" (IV, 329); he cannot partake of the many intrigues and must satisfy himself with the fact that "a boarding-house is a capital place for the study of human nature" (IV, 329). He practices "the good old Genevese principle of not sacrificing to appearances. This is an excellent principle—when you have the reality" (IV, 331). His clear observations establish our relationship with the characters, and the human nature he reveals is one that ruthlessly seeks a fanciful respectability by the most desperate means. He sees the impossibly despicable ways that limited people must use to maintain themselves, and in the contrast of the two daughters—Miss Sophy and Miss Aurora—he finds portrayed the end of these means and the difference between the American and the European tone.

Aurora wants to go to America because she is American-born, but also because she admires the freedom of Sophy, the American girl. Aurora admires her openness and independence but does not really understand her. What Aurora does not see about herself is that educated in Europe she has become a European girl; she could never survive in America. She says, strangely enough, "C'est mon rêve" (IV, 352) to go to Boston, but she does not know that in Boston she would not be understood because she is too consciously clever. She lies quite openly and simply to her mother as if it is what a girl does. In seeking to be like Sophy, she wants to be something that the narrator believes she cannot be. The point is suggested in the following dialogue between them.

"I have to pretend to be a *jeune fille*. I am not a jeune fille; no American girl is a jeune fille; an American girl is an intelligent, responsible creature. I have to pretend to be very innocent, but I am not very innocent."

"You don't pretend to be very innocent; you pretend to be—what shall I call it?—very wise."

"That's no pretence. I am wise."

"You are not an American girl," I ventured to observe.

My companion almost stopped, looking at me; there was a little flush in her cheek. "Voilà!" she said. "There's my false position. I want to be an American girl, and I'm not."

"Do you want me to tell you?" I went on. "An American girl wouldn't talk as you are talking now."

"Please tell me," said Aurora Church, with expressive eagerness. "How would she talk?"

"I can't tell you all the things an American girl would say, but I think I can tell you the things she wouldn't say. She wouldn't reason out her conduct, as you seem to me to do."

Aurora gave me the most flattering attention. "I see. She would be simpler. To do very simple things that are not at all simple—that is the American girl!"

I permitted myself a small explosion of hilarity. "I don't know whether you are a French girl, or what you are," I said, "but you are very witty."

"Ah, you mean that I strike false notes!" cried Aurora Church, sadly. "That's just what I want to avoid. I wish you would always tell me." (IV, 369)

The difficulty is that Aurora is an impossible combination. She is like a hybrid: she is born American and educated as a European. She cannot stand her mother's vulgar American interpretation of European propriety that does not allow her to know interesting people, only respectable people; but she could not stand for long the free and open flatness of Sophy's America. She is the desperate result bred of desperate means. Madame Beaurepas, after forty years of keeping a boardinghouse, says she knows what will happen: "Some fine morning—or evening—she will go off with a young man; probably with a young American" (IV, 361).

Mrs. Church is all intellect and propriety, and James clearly respects her for her brave attempt to make the most of little, but hers is a pretentious, materialistic vision—one no better than the Rucks', only less obvious. Her life necessitates countless ignoble moments, such as arguing with porters over fees, refusing to speak to those she thinks inferior—like the Rucks, demanding special wines that she has no right to, not knowing she is being deceived by her daughter. Mrs. Ruck is worse. She does nothing for her daughter but make her like herself. They are two of a kind. At least Mrs. Church does attempt to educate Aurora to a respectable and comfortable marriage, as horrible as a magistrate, a deputy, a "*gros bonnet*" will be to Aurora. If Mrs. Church too carefully cultivates her daughter, almost to the point of suffocation, Mrs. Ruck simply lets Sophy grow wild as she will. Sophy, the "wise" American woman Aurora seeks, is taught only how to buy, how to dress, and how to answer back. She has an independent mind, but to no purpose. She is taught by her mother to use men, and she uses Mr. Ruck mercilessly. She does not see, because her mother does not, that he is a sick man who must return to his business if he and it are to be saved. She and her mother do not see that without his business he and they are nothing. His money creates their reality. The narrator says, "The duty of an American husband and father is to keep them going. If he asks them how, that's his own affair. So, by way of not being mean, of being a good American husband and father, poor Ruck stands staring at bankruptcy" (IV, 377). This is the end that Sophy's means will bring.

Mr. Ruck is an unusual character for James, since he is a sympathetically portrayed American businessman. James acknowledges that Ruck has little education or refinement, but he is an honest, direct man who—day by day—loses everything he owns. Still he tries with dignity and humor to hold up his side. The side is in itself despicable—the subservient American husband who must produce the money—but his attempt is made with all the dignity his years are able to give him, with more dignity than one might expect him to have acquired in such a life. After learning of his complete financial ruin, he is last seen trying not to break down as his wife and daughter buy jewelry he cannot pay for.

M. Pigeonneau, the Frenchman, views the scene from a distance. It is all a game to be played, to be watched, to be recorded, but it is only a game to him. Nothing in life is serious; nothing is comic; nothing is really distinctive. Madame Beaurepas has one philosophy: " 'Je trouve que c'est déplacé!' " (IV, 330), I find it out of place. She has seen everything; everything has happened once in her house, but she does not let anything happen twice.

As for the narrator—what he sees is the story we read,

but that must be seen, in itself, as another vision of reality. James does suggest in the many events of the tale that take place in the closed garden of the pension and on the broad and open terrace of the English Garden—a little restaurant in Geneva—the contrast between the limited life of the Churches, who move from one pension to another, and the possible expanse of life that could be seen by those who are free, like the Rucks. However, Mr. Ruck turns his back on the view of the mountains and only contemplates his diminishing money; and his wife and daughter know only how to spend his money, not how to create a life with it. Perhaps James suggests in M. Pigeonneau's cynicism about life and his joy in women and Madame Beaurepas' flat acceptance of life some kind of ideal, the "Genevese principle of not sacrificing to appearances." However, they both seem so smugly set in the provincial city of Geneva, described as a step down from the real life of Paris and as the home of the dogmatic Calvin, that the drama of life passes them by, the drama the narrator observes in the Rucks and the Churches. For all their failure, the Americans are seen in some sort of movement. The tale suggests that it is better to be little like the Genevese than to be preposterous like the Rucks, but it also implies that much of what is little is also slight in what it sees and in what it possesses. The reader must ask: What does one make of these many visions of reality? Perhaps the lightest touch of the tale, and in some ways the truest, is that James does not finally answer the question. He only gives us the multiple insights of his artistic narrator and leaves the evaluation open.

"The Diary of a Man of Fifty" is a simpler story. An elderly British officer, who has gone to India and elsewhere as a soldier, records in his diary his return to Florence. Here he finds a young Englishman, Stanmer, in love with the daughter of the Italian woman whom the older man had loved but left because he questioned her quality and honor. He tries to persuade the young man that his situation is similar, but the young man marries his woman. The marriage works, and it becomes clear that she—like her mother perhaps—was only waiting for a man's protection to move out of an impossibly compromising situation. Before Stanmer leaves, he speaks to the older man.

> "Has it ever occurred to you that *you* may have made a great mistake?"
> "Oh yes; everything occurs to one sooner or later."
> That's what I said to him; but I didn't say that the question, pointed by his candid young countenance, had, for the moment, a greater force than it had ever had before.
> And then he asked me whether, as things had turned out, I myself had been so especially happy. (IV, 423)

And in a note after his marriage he says to the unnamed man of fifty: *"Things that involve a risk are like the Christian faith; they must be seen from the inside"* (IV, 423). The narrator's final entry in his diary is:

> *Was* I wrong—*was* it a mistake? Was I too cautious—too suspicious—too logical? Was it really a protector she needed—a man who might have helped her? Would it have been for his benefit to believe in her, and was her fault only that I had forsaken her? Was the poor woman very unhappy? God forgive me, how the questions come crowding in! If I marred her happiness, I certainly didn't make my own. And I might have made it—eh? That's a charming discovery for a man of my age! (IV, 425)

The conclusion seems easy to make and the story not difficult to understand. The narrator will not take the plunge, as Longmore in "Madame de Mauves" would not, and years later he is still confronted with the imaginative possibility and the painful reality. He has not seen life from the inside. However, the tale leaves a doubt. The narrator's life has been "a good deal alone" (IV, 395), but it has not been a bad life. Would it have been worse had he married, or is it worse not to have known at all his imagined possibilities than to have attempted to realize them and to have failed? Even reasoning thus, one must answer that it would have been better to have tried. The life of the narrator's mind could have been so much greater had he moved out, but it is limited by a refusal to see reality. In this story it is not reality that limits the mind, but the mind that has limited reality. James is not usually interested in a mind that sees less than reality possesses. When he is, the central character is generally a male like Longmore or Winterbourne—or perhaps the narrator in "Four Meetings." In James's fiction the cowards of mind and action are often the men, and it is left to the women to be of quality and character.

The tale continues to pose the multiple conflicts between imagination and reality. Yet even in writing such simple stories as "The Pension Beaurepas" and "The Diary of a Man of Fifty," James never simplifies this conflict. It is not only in the novels of the 1890's that James experiments with the levels of awareness in the mind and the points of view on reality that shape these levels. *What Maisie Knew, The Awkward Age, The Sacred Fount* are all foreshadowed. His tales ending this first period begin this examination, these experiments. The last tale of this early period is not a major work, but it is an intriguing examination and experiment, one that in another form, a form more dramatic, James will return to when he writes *The Awkward Age.*

"A Bundle of Letters" is just that—nine letters written from a Parisian pension by several people: Miranda Hope, an American girl from Bangor, Maine, traveling alone, is the principal correspondent and writes to her mother; Violet Ray, another American girl, traveling with her mother, writes to a friend in New York City; Louis Leverett, a mild-mannered Bostonian, an observer of life, writes to his friend Harvard Trement in Boston; Miss Evelyn Vane, a young English girl passing a short time in the pension, corresponds with Lady Augusta Fleming at Brighton; Léon Verdier, a Frenchman giving lessons while living in his cousin's pension, describes to Prosper Gobain in Lille the eccentric scene he observes; and Dr. Rudolf Staub corresponds with his German "Brother in Science" at Göttingen, Dr. Julius Hirsch, about the superficiality of the race of humans he observes in Paris.

The situation is obvious; the drama is in the inevitably conflicting points of view and interpretations of reality. James shows the characters passing judgments on themselves as they arrogantly and insensitively judge one another. On one level the tale is comic as each individual interprets what is seen only to satisfy his vanity and national pride. The opinions are preposterous and there is little concern with truth or objectivity, except in the most pathetic ways. The use of the epistolary form suggests the limitation of the vision: it is a tale of no communication, except in letters, a tale of fixed attitudes. On the second level, the tale is painful. Miranda tries to be the most objective, and most sincere, the most frank, but she has so much to learn that one realizes that she will never transcend the limitations of her background. Violet Ray is a spoiled American girl; like Sophy Ruck, she is Daisy Miller gone from bad to worse, and she sees only *her* American way, as Henrietta Stackpole will in *The Portrait of a Lady*. Louis Leverett is a charmingly ineffectual aesthete who sees as much of life as anyone would from a comfortable leather armchair. He is not really intolerant or unpleasant; he is somewhat like

Ralph Touchett, only lighter. Evelyn Vane is preposterous. Like Lord Warburton's sisters in *The Portrait of a Lady*, she sees exactly what her brother has told her to see. Léon Verdier is typically French and is all curiosity about how people could behave in a manner so unlike the French. The German, Dr. Rudolf Staub, is disgusted with the other nations and waits for the rational control of the Germans to assume power. He is the most frightening character for he is not just insensitive, he is also ruthless and brutal.

The situation is too clever to be serious, but the story is so well written that it is successful. James wants us to admit the existence of these conflicting visions of reality and to see the absurdity of insisting upon any one vision absolutely. He seems to say that these are not people of a sophisticated vision because in their limited arrogance they can judge only by their limitations. In these purposes he succeeds admirably, and by doing so presents his own relationship to reality: it is in a multifarious quality that we can only try to see rationally and to understand imaginatively. This occupation is endless for all of us, and especially for the artist.

The particularity of the observations and the breadth of viewpoints can be illustrated by quoting several sections from the letters. The precise detail set in the light tone is essential to the tale: the former gives the letters their vividness and suggests the narrow opinions that limit each writer, while the latter comments ironically on this limitation and suggests the pathetic undercurrent of vanity and insecurity.

> I do just exactly as I do in Bangor, and I find I do perfectly right; and at any rate, I don't care if I don't. I didn't come to Europe to lead a merely conventional life; I could do that at Bangor. You know I never *would* do it at Bangor, so it isn't likely I am going to make myself miserable over here. So long as I accomplish what I desire,

and make my money hold out, I shall regard the thing as a success. (IV, 429)

MIRANDA HOPE

It's father's theory that we are always running up bills, whereas a little observation would show him that we wear the same old *rags* FOR MONTHS. But father has no observation; he has nothing but theories. Mother and I, however, have, fortunately, a great deal of *practice*, and we succeeded in making him understand that we wouldn't budge from Paris, and that we would rather be chopped into small pieces than cross that dreadful ocean again. So, at last, he decided to go back alone, and to leave us here for three months. But, to show you how fussy he is, he refused to let us stay at the hotel, and insisted that we should go into a *family*. I don't know what put such an idea into his head, unless it was some advertisement that he saw in one of the American papers that are published here. (IV, 435)

VIOLET RAY

She is going to take Miss Travers, who has been with us so long, but who is only qualified for the younger children, to Hyères, and I believe some of the Kingscote servants. She has perfect confidence in Miss T.; it is only a pity she has such an odd name. Mamma thought of asking her if she would mind taking another when she came; but papa thought she might object. Lady Battledown makes all her governesses take the same name; she gives £5 more a year for the purpose. I forget what it is she calls them; I think it's Johnson (which to me always suggests a lady's maid). Governesses shouldn't have too pretty a name; they shouldn't have a nicer name than the family. (IV, 453)

EVELYN VANE

He is an illustration of the period of culture in which the faculty of appreciation has obtained such a preponderance over that of production that the latter sinks into a kind of rank sterility, and the mental condition becomes analogous to that of a malarious bog. I learn from him that there is an immense number of Americans exactly resembling him, and that the city of Boston, indeed, is almost exclusively composed of them. (He communicated this fact very proudly, as if it were greatly to the credit of his native country; little perceiving the truly sinister impression it made upon me.) (IV, 462–63)

DR. RUDOLF STAUB

These quotations do not include any by the aesthetic American, Louis Leverett, although the last is the German's comment on Leverett's un-Germanic approach to life. The irony of the German's remark is not in how untrue it is, but in the fact that Leverett is so atypical of America and yet thought to be so extraordinarily typical. Or is the irony in that Leverett *is* typical of his class and of the educated American, yet the German little realizes how unimportant that class is in America? Leverett makes several interesting remarks in his letter and he comes closest to James's own attitude. The main point of Leverett's letter is his ardent defense of "living life." Here are the first two paragraphs that suggest this concern:

I have carried out my plan, of which I gave you a hint in my last, and I only regret that I should not have done it before. It is human nature, after all, that is the most interesting thing in the world, and it only reveals itself to the truly earnest seeker. There is a want of earnestness in that life of hotels and railroad trains, which so many of our countrymen are content to lead in this strange Old World, and I was distressed to find how far I, myself, had been led along the dusty, beaten track. I had, however, constantly wanted to turn aside into more unfrequented ways; to plunge beneath the surface and see what I should discover. But the opportunity had always been missing; somehow, I never meet those opportunities that we hear about and read about—the things that happen to people in novels and biographies. And yet I am always on the watch to take advantage of any opening that may present itself; I am always looking out for experiences, for sensations—I might almost say for adventures.

The great thing is to *live*, you know—to feel, to be conscious of one's possibilities; not to pass through life mechanically and insensibly, like a letter through the post-office. There are times, my dear Harvard, when I feel as if I were really capable of everything—*capable de tout*, as they say here—of the greatest excesses as well as the greatest heroism. Oh, to be able to say that one has lived —*qu'on a vécu*, as they say here—that idea exercises an indefinable attraction for me. You will, perhaps, reply, it is easy to say it; but the thing is to make people believe you! And, then, I don't want any second-hand, spurious sensations; I want the knowledge that leaves a trace—that leaves strange scars and stains and reveries behind it! But I am afraid I shock you, perhaps even frighten you. (IV, 439–40)

The reference to plunging is again similar to the one by Longmore in "Madame de Mauves," as well as the remark by Eugene Pickering about himself in the tale of the same name. The concern is one that goes back to James's earliest tales. Leverett goes on to criticize Boston's lack of sympathy with the artistic temper—as James might have done—and to say that in Boston one cannot live aesthetically, sensuously, and that "the great thing [is] . . . to be free, to be frank, to be *naïf*" (IV, 440). He asks himself, "what is life but an art?" (IV, 441), and maintains he will not "shrink from carrying out my theory that the great thing is to *live*" (IV, 441). He mentions Balzac, "who never shrank from the reality" (IV, 441), and *Le Père Goriot*, and then Leverett makes the following remark:

I am much interested in the study of national types; in comparing, contrasting, seizing the strong points, the weak points, the point of view of each. It is interesting to shift one's point of view—to enter into strange, exotic ways of looking at life. (IV, 442)

Louis Leverett does nothing, although to do something is clearly what he desires. He simply compares the American females at the pension and finishes his letter. He seems to be endlessly amiable and instructive—to judge by the other letters that comment on him—but also to be totally ineffectual. His life of the mind, endlessly carried on, leads him nowhere. With all his intentions to live life, he sustains none at all. It is this failure that separates him from James, although James well understands the danger Leverett represents. It is Leverett's refusal to use his mind to sustain his life, to take the plunge and live in any form—in life or art—that makes the remarks of the German, although harsh, also just social criticism of the Boston intellectual. There *are*, indeed, certain limits to our subtle observations—as there are to our crass encounters with reality. We can only go so far either way without being ineffectual on one side or animalistic on the other, but we cannot stop long before these limits or we diminish the life that comes in the mind and the life that comes through the physically understood experience. We must move both ways in balance to reach a perspective on reality. It is a delicate, necessary balance. These letters suggest in their insensitive arrogance how difficult that balance is because of our limited vision.

Very late in James's own life, on March 21, 1914—two years before his death—James wrote to Henry Adams in reply to a melancholy letter. James had just sent Adams the second volume of *Notes of a Son and Brother*. James expresses his understanding of the tragedy in life, in the difference between the actual and the possible, but he pushes against this current his determination as an artist to see as much of life as he can. The letter, thrown back across the years, is the defense of an artist who saw so much of the pain that must exist in any life and understood that a means to live had to be found, a means broad and tolerant, yet certain of possible achievement in life's endless exploration of reality.

My dear Henry,

I have your melancholy outpouring of the 7th, and I know not how better to acknowledge it than by the full recognition of its unmitigated blackness. *Of course* we are lone survivors, of course the past that was our lives is at the bottom of an abyss—if the abyss *has* any bottom; of course, too, there's no use talking unless one particularly *wants* to. But the purpose, almost, of my printed divagations was to show you that one *can*, strange to say, still want to—or at least can behave as if one did. Behold me therefore so behaving—and apparently capable of continuing to do so. I still find my consciousness interesting—under *cultivation* of the interest. Cultivate it *with* me, dear Henry—that's what I hoped to make you do—to cultivate yours for all that it has in common with mine. *Why* mine yields an interest I don't know that I can tell you, but I don't challenge or quarrel with it—I encourage it with a ghastly grin. You see I still, in presence of life (or of what you deny to be such,) have reactions—as many as possible—and the book I sent you is a proof of them. It's, I suppose, because I am that queer monster, the artist, an obstinate finality, an inexhaustible sensibility. Hence the reactions—appearances, memories, many things, go on playing upon it with consequences that I note and "enjoy" (grim word!) noting. It all takes doing—and I *do*. I believe I shall do yet again—it is still an act of life. But you perform them still yourself—and I don't know what keeps me from calling your letter a charming one! There we are, and it's a blessing that you understand—I admit indeed alone—your all-faithful

Henry James [19]

As this letter indicates, as these last tales reveal, James leads us to an unusual point of view—one that is without absolutes, but one that is deeply committed to the observation of reality and the conscious exploration of life's imaginative possibilities. He seeks a balance between our idealism and the reality of the human condition. He leaves us in a difficult place, for he asks for a consciousness that is as fine in observation as it is active in response, yet he allows for no absolute judgments and prescribes no rules of procedure except intelligence, sensitivity, courage, and passion. We cannot expect to be told what is, nor to know that what is now will be so again. We are only sustained by the endless fascination of life's possibilities and by our hopeless but valiant attempt to artistically structure a course for ourselves. If one is an artist, James says in his letter to Adams and in his fiction, one is possessed by life; one cannot avoid responding. One is caught by reality and its shifting conditions, conditions that the imagination then structures into myriad possibilities. The process is not just "an act of life," as James says to Adams; it is *the* act of life, its very method of being.

Notes

Introduction

1. *The Complete Tales of Henry James*, ed. Leon Edel, 12 vols. (London, 1962–64). The text for this study is the English edition of the complete tales rather than the American one published by Lippincott, although the editions are similar and page references to one apply to the other. References to these texts will be by volume and page given in parentheses after the quoted material.

The reader interested in the publishing history of the tales is referred to the note at the end of each of the twelve volumes or to Leon Edel and Dan H. Laurence, *A Bibliography of Henry James*, 2nd ed., rev. (London, 1961).

James was one of twelve contributors to *The Whole Family* (1908), a novel with each chapter written by a different author. He published his contribution, "The Married Son," separately in *Harper's Bazaar* in June 1908. Rightly Mr. Edel does not include this in the collected tales, although it is sometimes considered as a short story, as James's contribution to this peculiar novel is so distinct from the rest.

2. *The Art of the Novel: Critical Prefaces by Henry James*, introd. Richard P. Blackmur (New York, 1934), p. 178; cited hereafter as *Prefaces*.

3. *Ibid.*, p. 139.

4. *Ibid.*, p. 139.

5. *Ibid.*, p. 181.

6. *Ibid.*, p. 220.

7. *Ibid.*, p. 220.

8. *Ibid.*, p. 180.

9. *Ibid.*, p. 231.

10. *Ibid.*, p. 172.

11. *Ibid.*, p. 263.

12. *Ibid.*, p. 201.

13. Marius Bewley, *The Eccentric Design: Form in the Classic American Novel* (New York, 1963), p. 229. Chapter IX in this book is called "Henry James and 'Life.'"

14. *Prefaces*, p. 202.

15. *Ibid.*, p. 202.

1 – The Apprentice Years – Life in America: 1864–1868

1. These technical points are noted in the study by Krishna Baldev Vaid, *Technique in the Tales of Henry James* (Cambridge, Mass., 1964), pp. 126–34.

2. Percy G. Adams, "Young Henry James and the Lesson of His Master Balzac," *Revue de Littérature Comparée* (July–September 1961), 458–67. Mr. Adams gives sources in Balzac for the following tales by James: "Poor Richard," "De Grey," "Gabrielle de Bergerac," "The Madonna of the Future," "The Sweetheart of M. Briseux," and "Eugene Pickering." The last of these tales was written in 1874; Adams finds little direct influence from Balzac on the later tales. "A Tragedy of Error" is not based upon a work by Balzac, but it clearly reveals the youthful enthusiasm James had for the French world his early master so effectively portrayed. See Marita Willet, "Henry James's Indebtedness to Balzac," *Revue de Littérature Comparée* (April–June 1967), 204–27, for the influence of *Le Père Goriot* on *The American*. See Leon Edel, *Henry James: The Untried Years* (Philadelphia, 1953), p. 216, for a comment on Balzac's influence on "A Tragedy of Error," and p. 163 for the early influence of Balzac on James. For other information on James's early life the writer has used Robert C. LeClair, *Young Henry James: 1843–1870* (New York, 1955).

3. Edel, *The Untried Years*, p. 239 ff. The present study is indebted throughout to Mr. Edel's biography and to his edition of the *Complete Tales*.

4. *Ibid.*, pp. 167–83. Mr. Edel's discussion of the relation-

ship between the injury and the war is reasonable, thorough, and, for me, conclusive.

5. "I shall take the liberty of asking the *Atlantic* people to send their letter of reject. or accept. to you. I cannot again stand the pressure of avowed authorship (for the present.) and their answer could not come here unobserved. Do not speak to Willie of this." From a letter to Thomas Sergeant Perry, March 25, 1864, in Virginia Harlow, *Thomas Sergeant Perry: A Biography and Letters to Perry from William, Henry, and Garth Wilkinson James* (Durham, North Carolina, 1950), p. 273.

6. Mr. Edel in *The Untried Years*, p. 65, makes this point in discussing James's decision to become a writer: "The evidence of Henry James's life points to a curiously paradoxical element in his personality: he was an active and masculine individual who finding direct action impossible—and with this direct expression of his individuality—realized this activity and individuality through a prodigiously creative and highly productive art, while remaining to all appearances passive in the extreme. The small boy cultivated a quiet aloofness; nothing would happen to him if he withdrew and used his eyes and his mind in that turbulent family. Inside the little mind great worlds were created, great achievements, great aggressions planned. For frustration, engendering aloofness, engendered also rebellion, and rebellion in turn had to be smothered to maintain his facade of passivity."

7. *The Letters of Henry James*, 2 vols., ed. Percy Lubbock (New York, 1920), I, 30–31; cited hereafter as *Letters I*.

8. All these tales appear in the first volume of Edel's *Complete Tales*.

9. *Henry James: Autobiography*, ed. Frederick W. Dupee (New York, 1956), p. 23.

10. Mr. Edel discusses certain actual events of James's life that probably influenced this tale: *The Untried Years*, pp. 226–38. In 1865 James was on vacation in the White Mountains with Oliver Wendell Holmes and John Chipman Gray, both apparently in uniform having just returned from the war. The three men paid court to the Temple girls, but particularly to Minny Temple. Mr. Edel notes that under

these circumstances—set in contrast to the two men returned from war—James did not appear to advantage, somewhat as Richard Maule, in the tale, does not next to the two Civil War officers. Mr. Edel also comments on the similar character grouping in life and in this tale—three individuals, one slightly an invalid, in love with one woman. This grouping is similar to one James uses in *Watch and Ward* and *The Portrait of a Lady*. Mr. Edel discusses the significance of this grouping of three suitors and one lady in his introduction to *Watch and Ward* (London, 1960), pp. 14–16.

11. See previous note and Edel, *The Untried Years*, pp. 226–38.

12. *Letters I*, p. 26. Clover Hooper later became Mrs. Henry Adams. She was a friend from the days at Cambridge.

13. Vaid, pp. 263–64. Mr. Vaid considers twenty-two of the first thirty-seven tales as first-person narratives. See also the introduction to *Eight Uncollected Tales of Henry James*, ed. Edna Kenton (New Burnswick, 1950), pp. 17–20, for a discussion of first-person narratives. This introduction also examines eight early tales, their foreshadowing of other tales, and the early use of certain Jamesian terms. Leon Edel, "Autobiography in Fiction: An Unpublished Review by Henry James," *Harvard Library Bulletin* (Spring 1957), 245–57, discusses James's early awareness of the problems of first-person narratives.

14. Mr. Edel in *The Untried Years*, pp. 237–38, sees what he calls "the vampire theme" as "enunciated for the first time" in "Poor Richard": one lover grows in health as the health, or life, of the other lover wanes. At one point in this tale Richard is ill with typhoid. As he recovers, he discovers Gertrude is ill. The theme is only suggested in the difficult relationship of Gertrude and Richard. James develops it more fully in two other tales: "De Grey" (1868) and "Longstaff's Marriage" (1878); it is also a major theme in *The Sacred Fount* (1901).

15. Marius Bewley, *The Eccentric Design: Form in the Classic American Novel* (New York, 1963), Chapter IX.

16. Henry James, *French Poets and Novelists*, introd. Leon Edel (New York, 1964), pp. 250–51.

17. For a discussion of the various techniques in these first eleven tales, and the next five, and for the relationship of these techniques to the later fiction, see Charles K. Fish, Jr., "Henry James and the Craft of Fiction: The Years of Exploration, 1864–1871," unpublished Ph.D. Dissertation, Princeton, 1963.

18. Ralph Barton Perry, *The Thought and Character of William James*, 2 vols. (Boston, 1935), I, 270–71.

19. *The Notebooks of Henry James*, eds. F. O. Matthiessen and Kenneth B. Murdock (New York, 1961), p. 18.

20. *The Art of the Novel: Critical Prefaces by Henry James*, introd. Richard P. Blackmur (New York, 1934), p. 5; cited hereafter as *Prefaces*.

21. Raymond D. Havens, "Henry James on One of His Early Stories," *American Literature* (March 1951), 131–33.

22. Edel, *The Untried Years*, p. 251.

23. Cornelia Pulsifer Kelley, *The Early Development of Henry James*, rev. (Urbana, 1965), p. 36.

24. Vaid, p. 133.

25. Edel, *The Untried Years*, p. 220.

26. James was asked to add an ending explaining that the marriage took place, which he did, reluctantly. He did not, as the ending shows, neatly conclude the tale. His letter on this matter reads in part: "As for adding a paragraph I should strongly object to it. It doesn't seem to me necessary. Silence on the subject will prove to the reader, I think, that the marriage *did* come off. I have little fear that the reader will miss a positive statement to that effect and the story closes in a more dramatic manner, to my apprehension, just as I have left it." *The Selected Letters of Henry James*, ed. Leon Edel (New York, 1960), pp. 59–60. This letter, James's indirect presentation of facts, and his use of irony are discussed by Charles K. Fish in "Indirection, Irony, and the Two Endings of James's 'The Story of a Masterpiece,'" *Modern Philology* (February 1965), 241–43. See LeClair, p. 399, for minor parallels between this tale and James's life.

27. Kelley, p. 81: "As a whole then *The Story of a Masterpiece* is inartistic and belongs to the explanatory type of fiction which James had been writing up to this time."

Edna Kenton, in her Introduction to *Eight Uncollected Tales*, p. 5, does point out relationships between this tale and "The Real Thing," "The Coxon Fund," and "The Liar."

28. What follows is not a discussion of Browning's poem, but an examination of the poem in relation to James's use of it in the tale. It should be pointed out that both the duchess and Marian "smile" at their painters, and that the husbands in both works read into this favor a moral element that appears to them in the portraits. Naturally Browning's husband is a nobleman of arrogant spite, which Lennox is not, but each shares a similar attitude towards the role of women. To avoid confusing the two works, it is best to consider that James uses Browning's situation, but gives it his own characterization.

2 – The Apprentice Years–Morality in Europe: 1868–1872

1. Leon Edel, *Henry James: The Conquest of London* (Philadelphia, 1962), p. 19 ff.

2. *The Art of the Novel: Critical Prefaces by Henry James*, introd. Richard P. Blackmur (New York, 1934), pp. 194–95; cited hereafter as *Prefaces*.

3. Leon Edel's Introduction to *Watch and Ward* (London, 1960) effectively discusses this work's slight significance in the James canon. Two further discussions of this novel that study its structure are J. A. Ward, *The Search for Form: Studies in the Structure of James's Fiction* (Chapel Hill, 1967), pp. 60–76, and Charles Fish, "Form and Revision: The Example of *Watch and Ward*," *Nineteenth-Century Fiction* (September 1967), 173–90.

4. Henry James, *Autobiography*, ed. Frederick W. Dupee (New York, 1956), pp. 123–24.

5. Virginia Harlow, *Thomas Sergeant Perry: A Biography and Letters to Perry from William, Henry, and Garth Wilkinson James* (Durham, N.C., 1950), pp. 270–71.

6. F. O. Matthiessen, *The James Family* (New York, 1947), pp. 10 and 21.

7. Henry Senior delivered a lecture in praise of socialism that he entitled "Socialism and Civilization," reprinted in Matthiessen, pp. 49–58.

8. *Prefaces*, p. 62.

9. Henry James Senior says that "the finiting principle in human life, the evil principle, is invariably that of selfhood or private personality; while the infiniting principle, the good principle consequently, is invariably that of society, or the broadest possible fellowship, equality, brotherhood, of man and man." This statement from *Society: The Redeemed Form of Man* (Boston, 1879), p. 314, is also quoted, except for the last phrase, in Jay Martin's *Harvests of Change: American Literature, 1865–1914* (Englewood Cliffs, New Jersey, 1967), p. 316. Mr. Martin's chapter on James covers his entire career, but considers some of the same ideas that are discussed here.

10. Henry wrote to William in 1907, after reading *Pragmatism*, that he "was lost in the wonder of the extent to which all my life I have . . . unconsciously pragmatised," and that he felt William was "immensely and universally *right*." Matthiessen, p. 343.

11. *The Selected Letters of Henry James*, ed. Leon Edel (New York, 1960), p. 203. The comment is made in reference to what another novelist is doing, but James is expressing his approval and agreement. James uses almost the same phrasing eleven years before in 1874 in the essay on Turgenev: "Something tells us, in this opening strain, that we are not invited to lend ear to the mere dead rattle that rises for ever from the surface of life." Henry James, *French Poets and Novelists*, introd. Leon Edel (New York, 1964), p. 237.

12. *Prefaces*, p. 45.

13. All eight are in the second volume of *The Complete Tales of Henry James*, ed. Leon Edel, 12 vols. (London, 1962–64). Certain other tales could have been included in this discussion, such as "De Grey," published in 1868 and concerned with young love, and even "A Problem" and "The Romance of Certain Old Clothes," also published in 1868, but these are excluded because they are tales primarily written to exploit the interest in the supernatural and are not essentially explorations of what could be James's personal considerations. "The Story of a Masterpiece" and "A Most Extraordinary Case" are so much better written that I place them before the period of uncertainty in James's life that the

eight tales represent, and, in fact, these two tales were published in January–February and April 1868, and were probably written earlier. Perhaps the point could be made in another way. "Osborne's Revenge," the first of the eight tales discussed in this chapter, appeared in July, 1868, during the same month as "De Grey," and might conceivably be placed with the first eleven tales discussed in Chapter 1, for James's next tale, "A Light Man," appeared in July 1869, one year after "Osborne's Revenge" and five months after James had gone to Europe and entered into this uncertain period in which he is set in neither America nor Europe. I do not put "Osborne's Revenge" with the earlier tales, however, for it seems much closer in theme and tone to "A Light Man" and the tales that follow.

14. Edel, Introduction to *Watch and Ward*, pp. 5–9.

15. See Edel, *Complete Tales*, II, 89.

16. The old man is both father and mother to the two young men, and his attachment to them seems peculiar. For a further comment on this point and a discussion of the importance of description to theme, see Charles K. Fish, "Description in Henry James's 'A Light Man,'" *English Language Notes* (March 1965), 211–15.

17. *Prefaces*, pp. 193–94 and 196.

18. Krishna Baldev Vaid, *Technique in the Tales of Henry James* (Cambridge, Mass., 1964), pp. 27–36. Mr. Vaid gives a more sympathetic interpretation of this tale. He considers it saved by the sane perspective of the narrator. It is possible to accept his general interpretation and still find the tale not one to be considered seriously. The narrator does give a rational perspective, but the vague and uncertain attitude James has towards his central character destroys the tale's effectiveness. Mr. Vaid is aware of this weakness, as he suggests on pp. 30–31.

19. Leon Edel, *Henry James: The Untried Years* (Philadelphia, 1953), pp. 335–36.

20. Harlow, pp. 284–85.

21. The comment from "A Passionate Pilgrim," with the reference to the haunted tenement, and these remarks about the moral reasons for James's decision to live abroad are of further interest when seen in relation to his late story, "The

Jolly Corner," in which the expatriate American returns to New York to his deserted house to confront the ghost of the man he would have been if he had remained in America.

22. Although the methods, materials, and conclusions are different from those found here, the articles and book by Quentin Anderson on the relationship between Henry James Senior and Henry Junior should be examined: "Henry James and the New Jerusalem," *Kenyon Review* (Autumn 1946), 515–66; "The Two Henry Jameses," *Scrutiny* (September 1947), 242–51; "Henry James, His Symbolism and His Critics," *Scrutiny* (December 1947), 12–19; *The American Henry James* (New Brunswick, 1957). William Troy's essay, "The New Generation," reprinted in *Henry James: A Collection of Critical Essays*, ed. Leon Edel (Englewood Cliffs, New Jersey, 1963), 79–91, examines James's legacy to the modern novel but also considers certain ideas similar to the ones presented in this chapter. The article by Robert J. Reilly, "Henry James and the Morality of Fiction," *American Literature* (March 1967), 1–30, uses different but importantly related material—the writings of William James—to reach conclusions similar to those in this chapter.

3—The International Style: 1873–1875

1. *The Art of the Novel: Critical Prefaces by Henry James*, introd. Richard P. Blackmur (New York, 1934), p. 15. One sees certain events in "Madame de Mauves" that are not seen by Longmore, but Longmore is like Rowland, James's central consciousness.

2. There are earlier tales that are concerned with the international theme—"A Passionate Pilgrim" being the most obvious—but it is not until "Madame de Mauves" that James is in control of his theme and his technique.

3. For a further examination of the relationship between these two works, see Benjamin C. Rountree, "James's Madame de Mauves and Madame de La Fayette's Princesse de Clèves," *Studies in Short Fiction* (Summer 1964), 264–71, and John Kenneth Simon, "A Study of Classical Gesture: Henry James and Madame de La Fayette," *Comparative Literature Studies*, III, 3 (1966), 273–83.

4. Henry James, *French Poets and Novelists*, introd. Leon

Edel (New York, 1964), pp. 197–210. James also mentions Flaubert's name in "Madame de Mauves" as an example of an author who is French in the same sense as the Baron de Mauves (III, 152).

5. Longmore's name has ambiguous overtones. Does he long for more of Madame de Mauves, or for more of life than he finds with her? Is he someone who always finds himself in situations in which he deliberately makes it impossible for himself to attain what he appears to want? James describes him on the first page of the tale as never choosing "the right-hand road without beginning to suspect after an hour's wayfaring that the left would have been the interesting one" (III, 123). It will be apparent throughout this discussion of "Madame de Mauves" that Longmore has many characteristics in common with Lambert Strether, just as Longmore's situation in the tale, in the central scene, resembles Strether's situation near the end of *The Ambassadors* when he encounters Chad and Madame de Vionnet in the country. One recognizes these parallels, but the particular elements of the two works are so distinctly different that the parallels are better simply noted than emphasized.

6. For a discussion of the structural relationships in this tale, see J. A. Ward, *The Search for Form: Studies in the Structure of James's Fiction* (Chapel Hill, 1967), pp. 77–94. For a discussion of "Madame de Mauves" that considers certain of these same ideas, see Marius Bewley, *The Eccentric Design: Form in the Classic American Novel* (New York, 1963), pp. 224–32. See also Robert C. McLean, "The 'Disappointed Observer' of *Madame de Mauves*," *Research Studies* (December 1965), 181–96. In another article Mr. McLean discusses the many obvious and important relationships between this tale and *The Ambassadors*. See "The Completed Vision: A Study of *Madame de Mauves* and *The Ambassadors*," *Modern Language Quarterly* (December 1967), 446–61.

7. *Roderick Hudson* is so relevant to a study of the early tales that it seemed necessary to consider it with them.

8. Henry James, *The Tragic Muse*, introd. Leon Edel (New York, 1960), p. 263. The Harper Torchbook edition is

used here as it is the most accessible and is based on the original 1890 text.

9. *Ibid.*, pp. 308–9.

10. *Atlantic Monthly,* XXXVI (October 1875), 404.

11. *Atlantic Monthly,* XXXVI (July 1875), 68.

12. *Atlantic Monthly,* XXXV (January 1875), 7.

13. *Ibid.*, p. 11.

14. *Atlantic Monthly,* XXXV (April 1875), 426.

15. *Atlantic Monthly,* XXXVI (August 1875), 130.

16. *Atlantic Monthly,* XXXVI (September 1875), 273–74.

17. See S. Gorley Putt, *Henry James: A Reader's Guide* (Ithaca, New York, 1966), pp. 43–44.

18. Krishna Baldev Vaid, *Technique in the Tales of Henry James* (Cambridge, Mass., 1964), p. 151; see S. Gorley Putt, *Scholars of the Heart: Essays in Criticism* (London, 1962), pp. 152–58, for a discussion of "Benvolio" and the theme of the divided person.

4—The Determined Artist: 1876–1880

1. Leon Edel, *Henry James: The Untried Years* (Philadelphia, 1953), pp. 313–36. See Chapter I for Minny Temple's early influence on the tale "Poor Richard."

2. *The Selected Letters of Henry James,* ed. Leon Edel (New York, 1960), p. 32, cited hereafter as *Selected Letters.*

3. *Ibid.*

4. *Henry James and H. G. Wells: A Record of Their Friendship, Their Debate on the Art of Fiction, and Their Quarrel,* eds. Leon Edel and Gordon N. Ray (Urbana, 1958), p. 267. This remark is made by James in 1915. See also R. P. Blackmur, "In the Country of the Blue," in *The Question of Henry James,* ed. F. W. Dupee (New York, 1945), 191–211. Blackmur sees the artist in James as a saint, the man "most wholly deprived." He considers the artist's life to be in the expression of his art and that the artist ceases to be an artist as he comes to life. The artist lives to express his vision, to be "in the country of the blue," and when he fails to express it, he can then be the subject of fiction. That is why James's stories of artists are about failure; had the

artist fully succeeded, he would have transcended the human condition of fiction. Of course, no one can so succeed.

5. This first major period also includes "Madame de Mauves" and *Roderick Hudson*, which are discussed in the previous chapter. I do not include *The American*, for although it is interesting as it establishes an American type, it is not a successful work, primarily for the reasons James gives in his Preface to this novel in the New York Edition. *The American* fails, finally, to keep the balance between reality and romance, particularly in the later part of the novel. By this remark I do not discount the value of this novel that Constance Rourke explains in *American Humor: A Study of the National Character* (New York, 1931), and that Richard Poirier examines in *The Comic Sense of Henry James: A Study of the Early Novels* (New York, 1960). I do not discuss here the other early novels since my study is of the tales; it only includes *Roderick Hudson* as a necessary extension of the ideas in "Madame de Mauves." Mr. Poirier's book, in particular on *The American, The Europeans,* and *Washington Square*, balances the opinions given here on the early tales.

6. F. R. Leavis does not think that James avoided this potential danger in the later fiction: "James paid the penalty of living too much as novelist, and not richly enough as a man. He paid the price, too, of his upbringing—of never having been allowed to take root in any community, so that, for all his intense critical interest in civilization, he never developed any sense of society as a system of functions and responsibilities. And he spent his life, when not at house-parties of a merely social kind (he was unaware, it would seem, of the Victorian country-house at its functional best), dining out and writing. The deep consciousness that he had no public and no hope of real critical attention would confirm the dispositions tending to life-impoverishment in his art. It is in this late period that the inherited symbolism assumes control, and we can see why this should be so: it moves into the place once occupied in force by the system of interests belonging to the novelist as novelist—the system of interests derived from his most vital experience. We can see too that

in coming so to power it both increases, and disguises from James, the separation of his art from life." "Henry James and the Function of Criticism," *Scrutiny* (Spring 1948), 102.

7. For a brief but effective summary of the discussion about this tale, see Leon Edel, *Henry James: The Conquest of London* (Philadelphia, 1962), pp. 302–12, and William T. Stafford, *James's 'Daisy Miller': The Story, The Play, The Critics* (New York, 1963).

8. *Selected Letters*, pp. 69–70, n. 1.

9. *Ibid.*, pp. 69–75.

10. *Ibid.*, p. 71.

11. *Ibid.*, p. 71.

12. *Ibid.*, p. 72.

13. *Ibid.*, p. 73.

14. *Ibid.*, p. 74.

15. *Ibid.*, p. 74.

16. Henry James, *Washington Square and The Europeans*, introd. R. P. Blackmur (New York, 1959), p. 11.

17. Robert J. Griffin in "Notes Toward an Exegesis: 'Four Meetings,'" *University of Kansas City Review* (Autumn 1962), 45–49, examines various levels of symbolic meaning in the tale and suggests that James considers Caroline Spencer a slight and pathetic woman whose romantic speculations about Europe are a substitute for her sexual frustration.

18. Edel, *The Conquest of London*, p. 417.

19. *Selected Letters*, pp. 169–70.

Selected Bibliography

Books on Henry James

Allen, Gay Wilson. *William James: A Bibliography*. New York, 1967.

Anderson, Quentin. *The American Henry James*. New Brunswick, 1957.

Andreas, Osborn. *Henry James and the Expanding Horizon: A Study of the Meaning and Basic Themes of James's Fiction*. Seattle, 1948.

Auchincloss, Louis. *Reflections of a Jacobite*. Boston, 1961.

Beach, Joseph Warren. *The Method of Henry James*. New Haven, 1918.

Bell, Millicent. *Edith Wharton & Henry James: The Story of Their Friendship*. New York, 1965.

Bewley, Marius. *The Complex Fate: Hawthorne, Henry James and Some Other American Writers*. London, 1952.

————. *The Eccentric Design: Form in the Classic American Novel*. New York, 1963.

Blackall, Jean Frantz. *Jamesian Ambiguity and "The Sacred Fount."* Ithaca, 1965.

Bowden, Edwin T. *The Themes of Henry James: A System of Observation Through the Visual Arts*. New Haven, 1956.

Brooks, Van Wyck. *The Pilgrimage of Henry James*. New York, 1925.

Cargill, Oscar. *The Novels of Henry James*. New York, 1961.

Dupee, F. W. *Henry James*. New York, 1965.

————, ed. *The Question of Henry James: A Collection of Critical Essays*. New York, 1945.

Edel, Leon, and Dan H. Laurence, eds. A *Bibliography of Henry James*, 2nd ed., rev. London, 1961.

Edel, Leon. *Henry James: The Untried Years*. Philadelphia, 1953.

———. *Henry James: The Conquest of London*. Philadelphia, 1962.

———. *Henry James: The Middle Years*. Philadelphia, 1962.

———. *The Prefaces of Henry James*. Paris, 1931.

Fiedler, Leslie A. *Love and Death in the American Novel*. New York, 1960.

Fish, Charles K., Jr. "Henry James and the Craft of Fiction: The Years of Exploration, 1864–1871." Unpublished Ph.D. Dissertation, Princeton, 1963.

Ford (Hueffer), Ford Madox. *Henry James: A Critical Study*. New York, 1915.

Gale, Robert L. *The Caught Image: Figurative Language in the Fiction of Henry James*. Chapel Hill, 1964.

———. *Plots and Characters in the Fiction of Henry James*. Hamden, Conn., 1965.

Geismar, Maxwell. *Henry James and the Jacobites*. Boston, 1963.

Grattan, C. Hartley. *The Three Jameses: A Family of Minds*. New York, 1962.

Harlow, Virginia. *Thomas Sergeant Perry: A Biography and Letters to Perry from William, Henry, and Garth Wilkinson James*. Durham, N.C., 1950.

Hoffmann, Charles G. *The Short Novels of Henry James*. New York, 1957.

Holder, Alan. *Three Voyagers in Search of Europe: A Study of Henry James, Ezra Pound, and T. S. Eliot*. Philadelphia, 1966.

Holland, Laurence Bedwell. *The Expense of Vision: Essays on the Craft of Henry James*. Princeton, 1964.

James, Alice. *Alice James: Her Brothers—Her Journal*, ed. Anna Robeson Burr. New York, 1934.

———. *The Diary of Alice James*, ed. Leon Edel. New York, 1964.

Kelley, Cornelia Pulsifer. *The Early Development of Henry James*, rev. ed. Urbana, 1965.

Knights, L. C. *Explorations: Essays in Criticism Mainly on the Literature of the Seventeenth Century.* London, 1946.

Krook, Dorothea. *The Ordeal of Consciousness in Henry James.* Cambridge, 1962.

Larrabee, Harold A., and Leon Edel. *Henry James, Sr., Class of 1830.* Schenectady, 1963.

Leavis, F. R. *The Great Tradition: George Eliot, Henry James, Joseph Conrad.* London, 1948.

Lebowitz, Naomi. *The Imagination of Loving: Henry James's Legacy to the Novel.* Detroit, 1965.

LeClair, Robert C. *Young Henry James: 1843–1870.* New York, 1955.

Lewis, R. W. B. *The American Adam: Innocence, Tragedy, and Tradition in the Nineteenth Century.* Chicago, 1965.

———. *Trials of the Word: Essays in American Literature and the Humanistic Tradition.* New Haven, 1965.

Leyburn, Ellen Douglass. *Strange Alloy: The Relation of Comedy to Tragedy in the Fiction of Henry James.* Chapel Hill, 1968.

Martin, Jay. *Harvests of Change: American Literature, 1865–1914.* Englewood Cliffs, N.J., 1967.

Matthiessen, F. O. *Henry James, The Major Phase.* New York, 1963.

———. *The James Family: Including Selections from the Writings of Henry James, Senior, William, Henry, & Alice James.* New York, 1961.

McElderry, Bruce R., Jr. *Henry James.* New Haven, 1965.

Mizener, Arthur. *The Sense of Life in the American Novel.* Boston, 1964.

Nowell-Smith, Simon. *The Legend of the Master.* New York, 1948.

Perry, Ralph Barton. *The Thought and Character of William James,* 2 volumes. Boston, 1935.

Poirier, Richard. *The Comic Sense of Henry James: A Study of the Early Novels.* New York, 1960.

———. *A World Elsewhere: The Place of Style in American Literature.* New York, 1966.

Putt, S. Gorley. *Henry James: A Reader's Guide.* Ithaca, New York, 1966.

————. *Scholars of the Heart*: *Essays in Criticism*. London, 1962.

Rahv, Philip. *Image and Idea*: *Fourteen Essays on Literary Themes*. New York, 1949.

Roberts, Morris. *Henry James's Criticism*. Cambridge, Mass., 1929.

Rourke, Constance. *American Humor*: *A Study of the National Character*. Garden City, 1931.

Sharp, Sister M. Corona, O.S.U. *The Confidante in Henry James*: *Evolution and Moral Value of a Fictive Character*. Notre Dame, Ind., 1963.

Smith, Henry Nash. "The Morals of Power: Business Enterprise as a Theme in Mid-Nineteenth-Century American Fiction," *Essays on American Literature in Honor of Jay B. Hubbell*, ed. Clarence Gohdes. Durham, North Carolina, 1967.

Stafford, William T., ed. *Perspectives on James's "The Portrait of a Lady"*: *A Collection of Critical Essays*. New York, 1967.

Stone, Edward. *The Battle and the Books*: *Some Aspects of Henry James*. Athens, 1964.

Stovall, Floyd, ed. *Eight American Authors*: *A Review of Research and Criticism*. New York, 1963.

Swan, Michael. *Henry James*. London, 1964.

Tanner, Tony. "Introduction" in *Henry James*: *Three Novels*: *The Europeans, The Spoils of Poynton, The Sacred Fount*. New York, 1968.

————, ed. *Henry James*: *Modern Judgements*. London, 1968.

————. *The Reign of Wonder*: *Naivety and Reality in American Literature*. Cambridge, 1965.

Vaid, Krishna Baldev. *Technique in the Tales of Henry James*. Cambridge, Mass., 1964.

Ward, J. A. *The Search for Form*: *Studies in the Structure of James's Fiction*. Chapel Hill, 1967.

Wegelin, Christof. *The Image of Europe in Henry James*. Dallas, 1958.

West, Rebecca. *Henry James*. New York, 1916.

Wiesenfarth, Joseph. *Henry James and the Dramatic Analogy: A Study of the Major Novels of the Middle Period. New York, 1963.

Winters, Yvor. Maule's Curse: Seven Studies in the History of American Obscurantism. Norfolk, 1938.

Articles on Henry James

Adams, Percy G. "Young Henry James and the Lesson of His Master Balzac," Revue de Littérature Comparée (July–September 1961), 458–67.

Anderson, Quentin. "Henry James and the New Jerusalem," Kenyon Review (Autumn 1946), 515–66.

———. "The Two Henry Jameses," Scrutiny (September 1947), 242–51.

———. "Henry James, His Symbolism and His Critics," Scrutiny (December 1947), 12–19.

Auchincloss, Louis. "The World of Henry James," Show (August 1964), 49–55.

Banta, Martha. "The House of the Seven Ushers and How They Grew: A Look at Jamesian Gothicism," Yale Review (Autumn 1967), 56–65.

Blackmur, R. P. "The Sacred Fount," Kenyon Review (Autumn 1942), 328–52.

Cecil, L. Moffitt. " 'Virtuous Attachment' in James' The Ambassadors," American Quarterly (Winter 1967), 719–24.

Daiches, David. "Sensibility and Technique (Preface to a Critique)," Kenyon Review (Autumn 1943), 568–79.

Edel, Leon. "The Architecture of Henry James' 'New York Edition,' " New England Quarterly (June 1951), 169–78.

———. "Henry James and Sir Sydney Warterlow: The Unpublished Diary of a British Diplomat," Times Literary Supplement (August 8, 1968), 844–45.

Edwards, Herbert. "Henry James and Ibsen," American Literature (May 1952), 208–23.

Firebaugh, Joseph J. "The Pragmatism of Henry James," Virginia Quarterly Review (Summer 1951), 419–35.

———. "A Schopenhauerian Novel: James's The Princess Casamassima," Nineteenth-Century Fiction (December 1958), 177–98.

Fish, Charles. "Form and Revision: The Example of *Watch and Ward*," *Nineteenth-Century Fiction* (September 1967), 173–90.

Fish, Charles K. "Indirection, Irony, and the Two Endings of James's 'The Story of a Masterpiece,'" *Modern Philology* (February 1965), 241–43.

——. "Description in Henry James's 'A Light Man,'" *English Language Notes* (March 1965), 211–15.

Gegenheimer, Albert Frank. "Early and Late Revisions in Henry James's 'A Passionate Pilgrim,'" *American Literature* (May 1951), 233–42.

Gibson, William M. "Metaphor in the Plot of 'The Ambassadors,'" *New England Quarterly* (September 1951), 291–305.

Goldsmith, Arnold L. "Henry James's Reconciliation of Free Will and Fatalism," *Nineteenth-Century Fiction* (September 1958), 109–26.

Griffin, Robert J. "Notes Toward an Exegesis: 'Four Meetings,'" *University of Kansas City Review* (Autumn 1962), 45–49.

Harris, Marie P. "Henry James, Lecturer," *American Literature* (November 1951), 302–14.

Havens, Raymond D. "Henry James on One of His Early Stories," *American Literature* (March 1951), 131–33.

Hopkins, Viola. "Gloriani and the Tides of Taste," *Nineteenth-Century Fiction* (June 1963), 65–71.

Howells, William Dean. "Henry James, Jr.," *Century Illustrated Monthly Magazine* (November 1882), 25–29.

Kaplan, Charles. "James' 'Madame de Mauves,'" *The Explicator* (February 1961).

Labrie, Ross. "Henry James's Idea of Consciousness," *American Literature* (January 1968), 517–29.

Leavis, F. R. "The Appreciation of Henry James," *Scrutiny* (Spring 1947), 229–37.

——. "Henry James and the Function of Criticism," *Scrutiny* (Spring 1948), 98–104.

——. "Henry James's First Novel," *Scrutiny* (September 1947), 295–301.

——. "The Novel as Dramatic Poem (III): 'The Europeans,'" *Scrutiny* (Summer 1948), 209–21.

————. " 'The Portrait of a Lady' Reprinted," *Scrutiny* (Summer 1948), 235–41.

Leavis, Q. D. "Henry James: The Stories," *Scrutiny* (Spring 1947), 223–29.

————. "The Institution of Henry James," *Scrutiny* (December 1947), 68–74.

Matthiessen, F. O. "Henry James' Portrait of the Artist," *Partisan Review* (Winter 1944), 71–87.

Mays, Milton A. "Henry James, or, The Beast in the Palace of Art," *American Literature* (January 1968), 467–87.

McElderry, B. R., Jr. "Hamlin Garland and Henry James," *American Literature* (January 1952), 433–46.

————. "The Uncollected Stories of Henry James," *American Literature* (November 1949), 279–91.

McLean, Robert C. "The Completed Vision: A Study of *Madame de Mauves* and *The Ambassadors*," *Modern Language Quarterly* (December 1967), 446–61.

————. "The 'Disappointed Observer' of *Madame de Mauves*," *Research Studies* (December 1965), 181–96.

Murray, Donald M. "Henry James and the English Reviewers, 1882–1890," *American Literature* (March 1952), 1–20.

Popkin, Henry. "The Two Theatres of Henry James," *New England Quarterly* (March 1951), 69–83.

Reilly, Robert J. "Henry James and the Morality of Fiction," *American Literature* (March 1967), 1–30.

Rogers, Robert. "The Beast in Henry James," *The American Imago* (Winter 1956), 427–54.

Rosenzweig, Saul. "The Ghost of Henry James," *Partisan Review* (Fall 1944), 436–55.

Rountree, Benjamin C. "James's Madame de Mauves and Madame de La Fayette's Princesse de Clèves," *Studies in Short Fiction* (Summer 1964), 264–71.

Sharp, Sister M. Corona, O.S.U. "Fatherhood in Henry James," *University of Toronto Quarterly* (April 1966), 279–92.

Shroeder, John W. "The Mothers of Henry James," *American Literature* (January 1951), 424–31.

Simon, John Kenneth. "A Study of Classical Gesture: Henry James and Madame de Lafayette," *Comparative Literature Studies*, III, 3 (1966), 273–83.

Stafford, William T. "Emerson and the James Family," *American Literature* (January 1953), 433–61.

Vivas, Eliseo. "Henry and William: (Two Notes)," *Kenyon Review* (Autumn 1943), 580–94.

Volpe, Edmond L. "James's Theory of Sex in Fiction," *Nineteenth-Century Fiction* (June 1958), 36–47.

Warren, Austin. "Myth and Dialectic in the Later Novels," *Kenyon Review* (Autumn 1943), 551–68.

Willet, Marita. "Henry James's Indebtedness to Balzac," *Revue de Littérature Comparée* (April–June 1967), 204–27.

Winner, Viola Hopkins. "The Artist and the Man in 'The Author of Beltraffio,'" *PMLA* (March 1968), 102–8.

———. "Pictorialism in Henry James's Theory of the Novel," *Criticism* (Winter 1967), 1–21.

Index